IN A NUTSHELL

OLD WISDOM THIS CATHOLIC NEVER KNEW

L.A. LEMKE

In a Nutshell: Old Wisdom This Catholic Never Knew

Copyright © 2017 by L.A. Lemke.

All rights reserved.

Published in the United States by L.H.S. Publishing.

Printed in the United States of America.

ISBN 978-0-9986248-0-8

*Dedicated to my two daughters,
beautiful gifts from God*

The skillful are not obvious
They appear to be simple-minded
Those who know this
know the patterns of [Wisdom]
To know [Wisdom] is [to have Power]
[This Power] moves all things
and [is called God].[1]

– Adapted from David R. Hawkins, M.D., Ph.D.

Contents

Author's Note | ix
Introduction | xi

One | Green Giant | 15
Two | Abundance | 21
Three | The Olden Days | 27
Four | Target Practice | 37
Five | Presents | 43
Six | Pre-Monday | 49
Seven | Lucky Number Seven | 55
Eight | Pacifier | 61
Nine | Planting | 69
Ten | Real-Life Examples | 75
Eleven | Dog Leash? | 83
Twelve | Time Out | 89
Thirteen | That's Life | 95
Fourteen | Forgiveness | 99
Fifteen | Closing | 105

Acknowledgements | 109
Discussion Guide | 111
Notes | 115
About the Author | 121

Author's Note

At the end of each chapter, I've included a piece of homework. Google the name of the song listed and choose the YouTube selection with the lyrics. Read along as the song plays; the words to these songs are based on God's Word and relate to the chapter.

Introduction

More than a decade ago, my life was turned upside down by an event that came out of nowhere. Although the details need not be disclosed, what I will say is that I was at rock bottom and had only one way to go. But how does a person dig themselves out of devastation all alone? Being a Catholic and a true believer in God, I went to church to find comfort. But week after week I wondered why I was there; I wasn't feeling closer to God or comforted by Him. *Why,* I thought, *do I go to Mass and rarely learn anything? Why is it the exception when I can actually relate to the homily? Why are the first and second readings so obscure? Can't we use a more modern translation of the readings?* Even Shakespeare's works are being translated so people can appreciate the works of art that they are. Therefore, I continued to search for comfort in my situation by speaking with friends.

One non-denominational Christian girlfriend told me I should read the Bible. She told me that she loves her church and that they read the Bible during their services. This was an anomaly to me—a woman who not only likes but loves her church and reading the Bible. I figured I couldn't lose anything by trying out her suggestions, so I decided to start reading the Bible.

It was then, at the age of thirty-eight, that I opened an old Bible I had received at a confirmation retreat in the eighth grade. It seemed Greek to me and I almost gave up as soon as I started. Instead, I called my Christian friend and told her my challenge with the Holy Bible. She directed me to buy a newer translation, one that uses more of today's verbiage. I bought a New Living Translation (NLT) Bible and I have never been the same.

I wrote this book after more than a decade of daily Bible study. At first, I had no clue what I was doing with this holy book in my lap; I just needed wisdom and started reading at whichever page my fingers opened to. It's amazing what happens when we are sincere about God's Word. He will direct us to the perfect Scripture, the perfect words for the moment. This book is about what I found. It holds the precious secrets God reveals only to those willing to look. God's riches and gifts to us cannot be intellectually discerned, and coming to the Word of God with an analytical mind will not help us understand our Lord. A mere acquisition of knowledge doesn't change the soul. The Lord's ways are counterintuitive to the world's ways. Not one biblical scholar will accurately reveal what God has to say unless that person has a humble and open heart to learn about the one true God.

Jesus said, "People who aren't spiritual can't receive these truths from God's spirit. It all sounds foolish to them and they can't understand it, for only those who are spiritual can understand what the Spirit means" (1 Cor 2:14 NLT). Another Bible verse related to this is, "O Father, Lord of heaven and earth, thank you for hiding these things from those who think themselves wise and clever, and for revealing it to the childlike. Yes, Father, it pleased you to do it this way!" (Mt 11:25-26 NLT).

The Bible can help you with anything in life (yes, anything!). You only have to be willing to spend time searching, thirsting, and waiting for our heavenly Father to open your eyes when He feels you are ready. It's all about God's timing and your desire to know Him. In a nutshell, the Bible illuminates how to handle all of our relationships in life: our relationships with our family, spouse, community, and even our enemies; our relationship to our job and how it needs its proper (but not excessive) place in our lives. In this book, I will discuss how God wants us to relate to our problems as well as our money. Most importantly, I will try to help you understand that a relationship with our Creator is paramount. Contrary to popular belief, you don't need a priest, a guardian angel, a saint, or the Virgin Mary to get you close to God. All you need to do is walk right up to Him yourself by taking hold of the Bible and sitting down to read. The Bible states, during the Crucifixion, that "Jesus breathed His last. And the veil of the temple was torn in two from top to bottom" (Mk 15:37-38 NASB). This means that Jesus opened the way to Himself; we no longer have anything separating us from our Lord. Since that day, we can approach Him ourselves through prayer and by reading the Bible. By doing this we can partake in all He promises us, and there are thousands of promises in the Bible.

If even I, the most oblivious person in the world when it came to the Bible, can now understand how wonderful our Father in Heaven is, and find extreme comfort and peace during the most horrific episode of my life, perhaps you can too. And in the process of getting to know our Lord, maybe, just maybe, you will find your true purpose in life. I did and I hope you will too. God promises us, "If you look for me wholeheartedly, you will find me" (Jer 29:13 NLT).

One

Green Giant

Have you ever wondered why we are on this earth? Have you ever been in a situation where the pain of life got so unbearable that you asked why we were even created? When I was in a terrible place, I felt a little abandoned, as many people feel when they experience hard times. I felt as if God created humans, took us in His hands Jolly-Green-Giant-style, tossed us into the air, and as we were landing on all seven continents, called out to us, "Good luck, I hope your life works out for you!" I was not in a happy place, and this feeling of shock and abandonment after a major life derailment made me look for answers.

Being raised in the Catholic Church with a faith in God, I immediately turned to my faith after my life as I knew it ended, but I wasn't getting what I needed. I went to Mass but didn't feel comforted. Instead, I wondered, "Is there something more out there that my church is not getting across to its people?" I wondered if the rules, traditions, and enactments of my church were getting in the way of actually knowing the Lord. I talked with Christian friends not of my faith and asked them for their opinions. One friend told me that we should live our lives in a way that brings glory to

God. *What in the world is that?* I thought. I had never learned that. *How are we supposed to give God glory in life if we really don't know what that entails?*

My religious upbringing consisted of going to church on Sundays, sometimes leaving immediately after communion. My family would pray a rote prayer before meals and at bedtime, and that was it. We really never discussed God. We never read the Bible, and if someone spoke about what was written within its pages, they were considered "Bible thumpers" in my neck of the woods. I did receive a Bible at an eighth grade confirmation retreat but I never opened it during the retreat, and when I got home I dropped it into a drawer never to be opened for decades! Despite all of this, my family felt that we were adequately "religious" by following the rules of the church. So when my friend said that our lives should be lived in a way that brings glory to God, it was as if she was speaking a foreign language! *Why do we even need to do this? After all, He is God; can't He give Himself glory? Was the reason for this devastation in my life that I didn't give God the glory He deserves?* These and countless other questions flooded my mind as my life took a drastic turn. I was confused and wanted answers so I turned to God himself, specifically His instruction manual to life, The Holy Bible. In fact, I opened the only Bible I owned, the one I received at that confirmation retreat many, many years ago.

When I first picked up that Bible I couldn't understand much of anything, but a Christian friend helped me find a translation that was more relatable. I bought it, started reading it, and I haven't been the same since. In order to summarize what I have discovered, I will use an analogy because analogies always help me when something is hard to comprehend.

There once was a father who decided to adopt a son. This father wanted to have a child to love and guide, to teach the ways of the Lord, and to give gifts that would make the child happy. The dad, of course, wanted the best for his child so that the boy would grow up to find purpose and avoid traveling on the wrong path. So the dad taught his son all that he knew. There were some consequences in life that could have been prevented by the father, but the son didn't consult with his dad and made his own choices. These choices led to negative consequences and the son realized that he should take counsel with his father in the future. When the son listened to the wisdom of his dad, he avoided many of Satan's traps and lies that can derail a great life. The dad was joyful to have a close relationship with his son and loved giving him gifts he would enjoy. When the son became a successful young man by following the wisdom he was taught, he realized that all the glory for his success should go to his dad, for it was his dad that led him along the best path in life.

Well, with our heavenly Father the scenario is the same. God created us for both our enjoyment and His. He wants to help us daily and therefore gave us the Bible and the Holy Spirit, which indwells every believer. Following the guidance from God's Word and the Holy Spirit, we will enter into a place of complete rest internally as we navigate our way in this crazy, fast-paced, and sometimes harsh world. Even if you have made a mess of your life due to poor choices, it doesn't matter—you can start to get your life back on track at any time. You were meant to live a happy, peace-filled, abundant life. The Bible says, "Delight yourself in the Lord, and He will give you the desires of your heart" (Ps 37:4 ESV). Best of all, when you decide to start listening to this guidance, you will be on the path of life taught in the Bible, instead of the path everyone else is following: one of temporary fun, too much work, and no lasting joy. The Lord states in the Bible, "My purpose is to give them a rich and satisfying life" (Jn 10:10b NLT). God doesn't make you wait until you get to heaven for the beautiful abundant life; who would want to follow the Lord if we couldn't enjoy the journey too? No, our rewards are daily as we decide each day to follow His lead. His instructions are in His promises and covenants found within the pages of the Bible: "The secret of the Lord is for those who fear Him, and He will make them know His covenant"* (Ps 25:14 NASB). The word *fear* in this verse is to have a healthy knowledge of the power of God. It is amazing to finally realize what God can do for us in this world if we walk beside Him in faith and follow all that He teaches us. You will begin to realize that we never need to be worried about anything in life; God is on our side. As long as our lives are in line with His teachings, we will defeat anything that is aligned with Satan—poverty, depression, loneliness, bitterness, anxiety, excessive work, substance abuse—the list goes on and on.

On the flip side, God also receives a reward when we follow His teachings and confess His power in our lives. When the people we associate with see our peace, joy, and hope for a great future, they will want those things for themselves too. The way we live and the changes others see will draw them to our heavenly Father. Now that is giving God the glory!

*Note: God's covenants (promises) can be conditional or non-conditional. When we follow God's conditions, He increases our blessings.

HOMEWORK:
Read the lyrics while listening to "Overcomer" by Mandisa[1]

SONG VERSE TO CONTEMPLATE:
"The same Man, the Great I am
The one who overcame death
He's living inside of you" [1]

GOD'S PROMISE:
"I can do all things through Him who strengthens me."
(Phil 4:13 NASB)

Two

Abundance

As I began to read the Bible, I received comfort for my situation and learned a great deal about how the Lord wants all of us to live our lives. Looking around my Catholic community, I realized that many people were suffering. Not all of them were suffering as I was, from a blow that tore life apart, but from the everyday drain of life that sucked them dry of joy, passion, and true happiness. This, I have come to know, is not the life the Lord wants for anyone.

God came to earth so that His followers could enjoy life to the fullest. He promises us, "I came that they may have life and have it abundantly" (Jn 10:10 ESV). An abundant life is a life in balance—a balance of work, rest, and time to enjoy our families and close friends. It is full of peace, joy, health, prosperity, and strength for the hard times that are inevitable in life. Somehow we as a society have all gotten off track and fall quite short of this life. The typical scenario today is not a balanced life at all. Families are always on the go with work, sporting events, daycare drop offs, heavy homework loads, and driving all around their spread-out communities to run their homes. Our work life has become our entire life and that is not how God intended it.

Let's take an example of dual-career families. If the husband and wife are both full-time employees, they probably work five days a week and a minimum of nine hours a day at their jobs (eight hours of work with an hour lunch). Due to the parents' schedules, the children in these families are putting in slightly longer days; they need to be dropped off at school first and picked up last. On average, the children of the people I observe in my community are in day care or school from 7:30am to 6:00pm on a daily basis, including during the summer. This means children are experiencing fifty-two hour "work" weeks! Did you catch that? Many children in two-career households are spending ten and a half hours a day away from home in a structured environment with lights, sounds, instruction and activities! I don't know about you, but when I am exposed to stimuli like lights, noise, and instruction for long periods of time, I get crabby, tired, burned out, and sick—and I am an adult! I didn't even mention that many children also have after school activities to go to beyond this incredibly long day. Most of us do not want this intensely busy life for our families, and neither does God. These schedules do not measure up to the abundant life the Lord wants for us, and thank God! We have the ability to change, with our Lord providing the way and the instruction manual to a balanced, happy, and peace-filled life.

Our instruction manual to life is the Bible. I have found that the Bible is the best-kept secret to the life we all want to live; maybe that is why it is the most popular book of all time. For some reason, many of us today don't read the Bible and it was never emphasized at all in the Catholic churches I attended in my life. Why? Probably because we don't think that a book written so long ago pertains to modern society. Remember, The Bible is the inspired word of God; who is better to give us advice on our lives than our Creator? Every problem we have today can be answered within the pages of this powerful book, and this is coming from a skeptic! The Bible says, "All Scripture is God-breathed and is useful for teaching" (2 Tim 3:16 NIV). If we don't look to the Bible as our instruction manual to life, our lives will follow mainstream ideals, which includes excessive work with little time for family.

There is dignity in hard work and a great work ethic. We should work at our jobs as if we are working for the Lord. "Whatever you do, work heartily, as for the Lord and not for men" (Col 3:23 ESV). We all know that nothing thrives when it is neglected. A life out of balance with excessive work, more often than not, is unfulfilling to the family members that live that way and could drive couples and families apart. God wants us to not only make a living, but to make a life as well. Nobody wants the money from hard work and long hours at their jobs to end up being split between two divorce attorneys. A divorce will require you to start over, which will use much of the hard-earned money that kept you from your family in the first place. It will also cause a lot of suffering to everyone, not least of these being the children. This is suffering that could be avoided if we follow God. By placing our trust in Him for a good life, instead of trusting in our jobs, bosses, stocks, and money, we will find that God never fails us. In Ephesians 1:19 (NLT) Paul states, "I also pray that you will understand the incredible greatness of God's power for us who believe in Him." As you seek the Lord, you will eventually understand how God can help you in life. When you put your trust in God's word and seek Him first, He will guide you to the best job for you and your family. But we are warned, "Don't love money; be satisfied with what you have. For God has said, 'I will never fail you. I will never abandon you'" (Heb 13:5 NLT). "For where your treasure is, there your heart will be also" (Mt 6:21 NIV). Our treasure should be relationships; a relationship with God deserves to be first. Then, remembering what God teaches us, we will know that family should be second and career third. Nothing should come before God's people. When you prioritize your life God's way and trust Him to take care of your family, in the end you will have a beautiful, fulfilling, and abundant life. Isn't that what we all want? "Those who know your name trust in you, for you, O Lord, do not abandon those who search for you" (Ps 9:10 NLT).

HOMEWORK:
Read the lyrics while listening to "Lose My Soul" by Tobymac[7]

SONG VERSE TO CONTEMPLATE:
"Everything I see draws me,
Though it's only in you that I can truly see that it's a feast for the eyes–a low blow to purpose.
And I'm a little kid at a three ring circus."[7]

GOD'S PROMISE:
"Take delight in the Lord, and He will give you the desires of your heart." (Ps 37:4 NIV)

Three

The Olden Days

Through the wisdom in the Bible, I have come to understand that the whole foundation of Christianity lies on the fact that God wants to help and have a relationship with the very people He created. We participate in this relationship by praying directly to Him. The Bible says that "In Him and through faith in Him we may approach God with freedom and confidence" (Eph 3:12 NIV). The Lord wants us to personally experience the gifts of being His followers and become privy to His wisdom, power, blessings, and help at all times. When I made this realization, it proved to be true in my life and it can also be true in yours. The secret to receiving these benefits is to commit your life to fully following the Lord.

Let's back up and lay a foundation so you can understand that all Christian followers of God have a reliable, bountiful source of unending supply through our Lord in heaven. God says, "I love those who love me, and those who seek me diligently find me. Riches and honor are with me, enduring wealth and righteousness. My fruit is better than gold" (Prov 8:17-19 ESV). This is a promise from the Lord. This promise, the one that leads to our abundant life, ironically starts with the harshest story of all, the horrendous way Jesus died, so we will start there.

Jesus came to earth as a man like us, suffering from ridicule and hate. During His time here on earth, He walked among people teaching them about compassion, humility, love, forgiveness, and how to follow Him. He turned water into wine, healed the sick, brought the dead back to life, produced manna from heaven, fed five thousand people with two fish and five loaves of bread, and performed many other miracles. Yet people continued to think of Jesus as an outcast who needed to be eliminated. Then, at the hands of Pontius Pilot, Jesus suffered a horrendous death, preceded by the task of dragging His cross up a hill while being beaten, mocked, and starved. He was then nailed to that cross. While He was hanging on the cross and suffering, Jesus cried out to His father, "My God, my God, why have you abandoned me?" (Mt 27:46b NLT).

Jesus chose to go through a traumatic experience here on earth just as many of us experience. He wanted to let us know that He has been there but now, through His death and resurrection, He is ever present to help us. He knew our lives would be hard; Satan is in the world doing nasty works that sometimes make our lives hell on earth. We need to know that God is available to help and guide us to the right path in life. The key is to believe in Him and trust Him. Christ's death and resurrection, which we celebrate every Easter, have significant meaning! God died so that He could live on within us, to help us with His power and guide us to a great life. The Bible states, "Nevertheless, I tell you the truth: it is to your advantage that I go away, for if I do not go away, the Helper [Holy Spirit] will not come to you. But if I go, I will send him to you" (Jn 16:7 ESV). The Holy Spirit is the power of God; this power lives inside all believers and we can call on it to help us. It gives us extreme peace, even when things are crumbling around us. It gives us strength to get through tremendously hard days with little sleep or help from others. The Holy Spirit can heal if we truly believe. The Lord made blind men see, cured many lifelong diseases for His followers, and even raised Lazarus from the dead in biblical times. The Bible states that "Jesus Christ is the same yesterday, today, and forever" (Heb 13:8 NLT). This verse tells us that although we haven't walked directly with Jesus as His followers did in biblical times, His power is still available. But it's only here for those who believe and live their lives according to His teachings.

God gave us life so that we could enjoy it and fulfill the purpose He has for each one of us. When we become like children and simply accept that He is our perfect parent who is with us all of the time through the Holy Spirit, we will experience His presence and His will for our lives. The Bible describes this trusting attitude as entering the Kingdom of Heaven when Jesus says, "I tell you the truth, unless you turn from your sin and become like little children, you will never get into the Kingdom of Heaven" (Mt 18:3 NLT). Why does the Bible use children in this verse? Because children believe everything they are told. God wants us to have this same open mind to His teachings—we need to believe what He is telling us through His Word. When we live life God's way, we open ourselves up to direct communication with our heavenly Father. We can receive answered prayers in all aspects of our lives: our health, our source of income, our relationship issues, everything! When you simply trust our Lord and live life by His teachings, your life will change for the better. The second part of that verse talks about entering the Kingdom of Heaven. The Kingdom is a spiritual place here on earth that you "step into," so to speak, when your life is aligned with the Lord. In the Kingdom of God, you are at rest, your prayers can be answered, and you feel at peace even if you are going through a tough situation. Entering this Kingdom involves an unveiling or stepping out of the kingdom of darkness; you finally realize how powerful God is and there is no fear in any situation. The Bible promises, "Whenever someone turns to the Lord, the veil is taken away" (2 Cor 3:16 NLT). Gaining wisdom from God does not require perfection; it requires a true heartfelt desire. Paul writes that the gospel "is hidden only from people who are perishing. Satan, who is the god of this world, has blinded the minds of those who don't believe. They are unable to see the glorious light of the Good News. They don't understand this message" (2 Cor 4:3-4 NLT). In other words, by following Satan's lies or refusing to believe in all that God wants for us, we will never know the magnificence of what God can do in our lives. Profound!

Many people have a horrible thought that the Lord is watching us, waiting to punish us when we mess up. But Scripture sets the record straight when it says, "for the Son of man did not come to destroy men's lives, but to save them" (Lk 9:56a NASB). Please keep in mind that our Lord loves each one of us more than our very own spouse, child, parent, or good friend does. He is looking out for our best interest and wants us to spend life in His kingdom on earth first and then in heaven. When we choose our way and not the way the Holy Spirit tells us, we suffer the natural consequences of that choice, but we can get back on track. God is always joyfully waiting for us to walk toward Him.

Many people don't realize that they are following Satan and his lies. One of the most alluring lies of Satan is that money is of utmost importance. Satan wants us to believe that money will help us attain everything we need and want in life, and that with money, our lives will be stress free and full of fun. He entices us with the thoughts of having nice things—beautiful houses, expensive toys, a big retirement portfolio, a jam-packed closet, and self-importance. Some of Satan's lies tell us that we need more money or we won't be able to retire; that we need to be recognized, so we should work excessively to climb up the corporate ladder; or, worst of all, that we shouldn't worry about our kids, because they don't really miss us when we work excessively, and children don't need much attention because they're resilient. These are definitely lies! They are intended to keep us busy and striving for anything other than solid relationships with our Father in heaven and our family members. We need to realize that everything we need can be found in a relationship with God. Deuteronomy 4:31 reminds us, "For the Lord your God is a compassionate God; He will not fail you nor destroy you" (Deut 4:31a NASB). Finding and following God's wisdom is the key that opens the doors to everything we need and desire. The Bible states, "Today I am giving you the choice between a blessing and a curse! You will be blessed if you obey the commands of the Lord your God that I am giving you today. But you will be cursed if you reject the commands of the Lord your God and turn away from Him and worship gods you have not known before." (Deut 11:26-28 NLT). Other "gods," also called idols, refer to things like money, materialism, beauty, or fame—anything that you seek wholeheartedly.

God did not create us to work an insane schedule. He chose to place us in this world to help us and to bless us so that we can enjoy our lives and, in turn, help and bless others. The close relationship with God that we receive when we read the wisdom of the Bible will give us more than we could ever ask for. God doesn't want only the rich to live an abundant life or for those who have not been gifted with a great income to suffer. Those with meager salaries may never make ends meet without God directing their steps. Lower income families do have an advantage if they are followers of God, however. Their faith in His provision will bestow upon them more blessings than those who have little faith and rely on their money. The Bible says, "Has not God chosen those who are poor in the eyes of the world to be rich in faith and to inherit the kingdom He promised those who love Him?" (Jas 2:5b NIV). Once again, the Kingdom of God means to experience all of God's gifts and help in this present age. The Bible says that "the kingdom of God is at hand" (Mk 1:15 ESV). Webster's definition of *at hand* is "nearby," "within reach," or "ready for use." This is profound! We don't have to wait to get to heaven in order to experience bountiful blessings and help in all aspects of our lives. God's help and blessings are for now, today, and always if we believe and follow His teachings. The book of Daniel states, "It is He who reveals the profound and hidden things" (Dan 2:22 NASB). God can give you an idea for a home-based business, a blog, or a book. He could lead you to a company where your talents are used to the fullest and you are completely fulfilled in your work. The Lord can bless your work in a way that benefits His world without sacrificing time with the people you love.

The Lord should be the foundation of our lives. Anything built on top of a foundation based on anything else will fade away. Jesus said,

"Everyone then who hears these words of mine and does them will be like a wise man who built his house on the rock. And the rain fell, and the floods came, and the winds blew and beat on that house, but it did not fall, because it had been founded on the rock. And everyone who hears these words of mine and does not do them will be like a foolish man who built his house on the sand. And the rain fell, and the floods came, and the winds blew and beat against that house, and it fell, and great was the fall of it" (Mt 7:24-27 ESV).

So you can try to build your life around what you want, chasing after your dreams. But if it doesn't fall in line with the Word of God, eventually it will come to a sudden halt. Bible says, "Seek the kingdom of God above all else, and live righteously, and He will give you everything you need" (Mt 6:33 NLT). This verse simply means to seek what God deems important; a relationship with Him should be first and foremost, not money. In finding this, your faith in God will be rewarded with whatever it is that you need. "For the pagan world runs after such things, and your Father knows that you need them" (Lk 12:30 NIV). The Lord assures us by saying, "Beloved, I pray that you may prosper in all things and be in health, just as your soul prospers" (3 John 1:2 NKJV). Our soul prospers when we are in touch with God, read His word, and follow His teachings.

In order to get started on your God-centered life, you need to make time for God every day. Buy a Bible that has a translation you can understand and start reading. Hebrews 11:6 tells us that God "rewards those who earnestly seek Him" (Heb 11:6 NIV). If you are putting Him first in your life, God will teach you how to slow down and reprioritize your life as well as the lives of your family members. A family life that follows God and His teachings is prioritized when the physical, mental, and emotional needs of family members are second only to time spent in His Word. This is a life that covets family time and prioritizes time to reconnect after each and every day. It is a life that treats God as an ever-present helper to ease burdens in the tough times. It is also a thankful life, one in which family members are truly cognizant of all of the blessings they already have. They know that even more blessings and help will become available as they keep their relationship with God a number-one priority.

It is possible in this world to make a good living without sacrificing your family time. It is possible to get off the treadmill of life and live a more sane existence. "For what will it profit a man if he gains the whole world and forfeits his soul?" (Mt 16:26a ESV). God gave us enough time in each day to accomplish what is truly important. When we give our life over to God, He directs us to put our lives in balance. Let us all try to do this so that our families, marriages, and homes are strong and healthy respites for our souls to grow in the likeness of our Creator. Remember, we are promised that "no good thing will He withhold from them that walk uprightly" (Ps 84:11b KJV). We walk uprightly when we prioritize our lives as God wishes us to and follow His teachings about how to live life. This shows our trust in the Lord and He never fails to bless a person who trusts in Him.

———————

HOMEWORK:
Read the lyrics while listening to "Lead Me" by Sanctus Real[1]

SONG VERSE TO CONTEMPLATE:
*"Don't want to leave them hungry for love,
Chasing things that I could give up"*[1]

GOD'S PROMISE:
If you give up anything that takes your eyes off of me, I will repay you in abundance.

Four

Target Practice

As I was reading Scripture to enrich my faith, I came across so many wonderful benefits for all of us in the Bible. For instance, I love the twenty-eighth chapter in Deuteronomy; I liken it to hitting the bull's eye of life! This chapter, which is worth stopping to read right now, reveals the blessings the Lord gives us for following His commandments and teachings. God did not abolish these commandments when He came to earth. We still need to keep them, even today, but the Lord will help us apply them to our lives. Let's start by reviewing the Ten Commandments:

1. You shall have no other gods before me.
2. You shall not make for yourselves any idol and worship it.
3. You shall not take the Lord's name in vain.
4. You shall keep the Sabbath day holy.
5. You shall honor/respect your father and mother.
6. You shall not kill.
7. You shall not commit adultery.
8. You shall not steal.
9. You shall not give false witness against your neighbor.

10. You shall not covet your neighbor's goods, house, wife, or anything your neighbor has. (Ex 20:1-17)

Over the last decade or so I have come to realize, for the first time in my life, that the Ten Commandments are all about love (yes, love!) and not rules and punishment. By following these commandments, we are committing our lives to following God who guides us to a life that supports our loving relationships. God then shows His love for us by blessing us for following His commandments. This act of obedience to God brings a sense of peace and happiness to our lives and saves us from the natural consequences of sin. All of the negative behaviors listed in the Ten Commandments lead to missing out on love at the very least and death at the very worst. If we break any of the Ten Commandments, we are sinning; this puts a barrier between us and the greatest source of love in our lives, our Father in heaven. This barrier lasts until we repent and change our ways: "We know that God does not listen to sinners, but He is ready to hear those who worship Him and do His will" (Jn 9:31 NLT).

By the way, the word *sin* has been really misconstrued over the years. We are told in the Bible that we are born sinners. Psalm 51:5 says, "Surely I was sinful at birth, sinful from the time my mother conceived me" (NIV). Really? A beautiful newborn baby is a sinner that needs to be baptized to wash away his sin? That never sat well with me. Here we are on this earth: we didn't choose to be born, and then we are slapped with a negative label the minute the nurse writes our birth time down in our medical record. How is it that *we* have to be responsible for all of our choices in life—the good, the bad, and the ugly? No one else takes the blame for our mistakes and yet we get labeled as sinners as a newborn because Adam and Eve sinned? This one took some time to understand but eventually God gave me the wisdom to discern the truth.

First of all, the word *sin* is best described in a book I read that states, "Sin means to miss the mark as an archer misses a target, so to sin means to miss the *point* of human existence. It means to live unskillfully, blindly and thus suffer and cause suffering."[1] The author goes on to say that sin is just a dysfunction of humans. Okay, so by our very nature we know that we do not possess the qualities of God. He is omniscient, omnipotent, and omnipresent, so as human beings we will always "miss the mark" without God; this is the meaning of original sin. God wants us to seek Him for direction into His kingdom (our best life), instead of acting like humans by following our feelings at any given moment. The Bible says, "The Lord does not let the righteous go hungry, but He thwarts the craving of the wicked" (Prov 10:3 NIV). In other words, when we are tempted to follow Satan's lures instead of listening to the Holy Spirit living within us, we are setting ourselves up for disappointment and we will continue to yearn for something to satisfy us. I have learned that only what God wants for us will satisfy us in the long term. In order to illustrate how following Satan can mess up our lives, let's use an example that most of us in today's society can relate to.

Let's assume that many people want to be in a loving relationship and settled into a marriage one day. As a dating relationship progresses, some people push aside their morals and standards in order to keep the other person happy. For instance, a person may feel the need to drink more alcohol or do drugs or engage in premarital sex when this is contrary to the teachings of the Lord. Some do this to hold on to a relationship that they think is "The One." This is making a choice based on fear, and there is no fear when

God is involved in the union. So when we do this, we are making a god out of a relationship instead of trusting God to keep us in peace while we wait on His timing and the person who is best for us to come into our lives. "Do not be deceived: 'Bad company corrupts good morals'" (1 Cor 15:33 NASB). We have to feel confident, even in this day and age, that God will bring us someone who will respect our standards and feel honored to be with a person who plans to keep sacred what is sacred. If we make relationship decisions based on fear, we "miss the mark," so to speak, by running ahead of God's will for our lives and this will cause us to suffer the natural consequences—consequences like unhappiness in our souls or a relationship with the wrong person and then backtracking to try and get it right. So sin means that we, as humans, are inclined to miss the mark in life unless we listen to God directing our steps. We need to experience death of our human targets and be born of the spirit, or "born again," when we are ready to accept that without God influencing our decisions, life will be messy, sometimes excruciatingly painful, and have no lasting joy. The Lord assures us, "I will guide you along the best pathway for your life. I will advise you and watch over you" (Ps 32:8 NLT). Remember to turn to God for help in all of your decisions. God is a loving Father who wants to bless us profusely so He gave us knowledge of how to live life. It's never too late to turn toward God; He is waiting for you to start having sustained joy in your life. What are you waiting for?

HOMEWORK:
Read the lyrics while listening to "Beautiful" by Dan Bremnes.[2]

SONG VERSE TO CONTEMPLATE:
*"Lord you know you've opened my eyes
Shown me things that I can't see on my own"*[2]

GOD'S PROMISE:
"Call to me and I will answer you. And I will show you great and wonderful things which you do not know."
(Jer 33:3 NLV)

Five

Presents

Although I was taught the Ten Commandments as a child growing up in the Catholic Church, we didn't dwell on them in Wednesday Catholic religion class. I didn't quite understand some of them at the time, like the commandment "You shall have no other gods before me" (Ex 20:3 NIV). But now, reading them as an adult who is digging deep to understand God and His word, the Lord has opened my eyes to understanding. God impressed upon my heart that breaking any of the commandments just harms us in the long run. I want to enjoy all of the blessings that I mentioned in the 28th chapter of Deuteronomy, and I am sure everyone feels the same. The chapter delineates what we get if we follow the Lord's teachings.

In a nutshell, the twenty-eighth chapter of Deuteronomy states that if you honor God's commandments and teachings, you will be blessed in the city and blessed in the country; you will be blessed coming in and blessed going out; "the fruit of your womb will be blessed;" the work of your hands will be blessed; your baskets will be overflowing; you will be the head and not the tail; you will lend and not borrow; the enemies that rise up against you will be defeated before you; and "the Lord will guarantee a blessing on everything you do" (Deut 28:1-12 NIV; 28:8 NLT).

Wow, that is quite a list! It seems too good to be true—in fact, that is exactly what I thought when I first read this chapter in Deuteronomy. But after years (yes, years!) of studying the Bible, I now know through experience that these promises given to us by God are trustworthy and real as we walk in the ways of the Lord.

What does it look like to walk in the ways of the Lord? you might ask. It means to first and foremost develop a daily, personal relationship with God through reading His Word. He will then direct you to the way you should carry out your life. It may take a long time to change things about yourself and your lifestyle, but God will help you. It takes great faith to go against mainstream lifestyles and live a life trusting God and following His teachings. This is one of the reasons we are guaranteed such great rewards. Look at the verse, "The Lord will guarantee a blessing on everything you do" (Deut 28:28 NLT). Another verse says, "The Lord your God will then make you successful in everything that you do" (Deut 30:9 NLT).What kind of job would you do if you knew that it would succeed? Would you spend more time making a difference in this world and less time on the treadmill of life chasing after money and/or recognition? God's world is perfectly ordered for His glory and our enjoyment. Why wouldn't God help us if we are sincerely seeking after Him and aligning our lives with His teachings? The Bible states, "But godliness with contentment is great gain" (1 Tim 6:6 KVJ) Perhaps, knowing this, you might slow down the frantic pace of your life. Maybe you'll take a job that is in tune with the gifts God gave you. I am sure our passions for certain work or hobbies aren't an accident. The talents God gave us such as photography, sewing, reading, coaching, landscape design, or business acumen don't need to sit idle as we make a living. If you decide to earn a more sane living for the sake of your family and use your gifts and talents instead of chasing after money, you will be aligning your life as God teaches. When God sees your faith and trust in Him, He will take care of you. The Bible states, "You will lend...but you will never need to borrow...the Lord will make you the head and not the tail," (Deut 28:12b-13 NLT) and "The fruit of your womb will be blessed" (Deut 28:4 NIV). Think about this for a moment. If you start a photography business you will be the "head" of it. If you set sane work hours, the fruit of your womb (your children) will be blessed because you will be home at a decent hour. Doesn't this all fall into place? Doesn't this all make sense? God's world is perfect, and the life we create for ourselves by relying on our own limited perspective is not. A family friendly work life is available for all believers, and our children will be blessed as we follow the Lord. The Bible teaches us that if you want to keep your life you have to give up your idea of it and turn to the Lord, following His lead. For instance, if you give up an expensive home to downsize so a parent can stay at home with the children, or if you give up a job with crazy work hours and you change to a job with more family friendly hours, God will reward you in this *present* age. You will be honoring His teachings. Remember the verse that said, "the kingdom of God is at hand" (Mark

1:15 ESV)? We don't need to wait until we get to heaven to experience an amazing life. God's provision is for now: He blesses now and performs miracles now. His Kingdom is alive and well for those willing to find it.

God gave me the idea to write this very book after I sincerely decided to put every aspect of my life in line with His teachings and remove all known, repeated sin from my life. I am not saying that I am perfect, but God knows my heart and He knows I am a true follower. What God can do in your life is far greater than what you can achieve for yourself. My hope in writing this book is that you realize God wants our priorities straight and by placing Him first we will be rewarded with a balanced life and multiple blessings. If you think about it logically, what god would allow only massive amounts of work with little time for loved ones to be the right path or the only way to make a prosperous living? How can we help and bless others if we are so busy? How can we enjoy His beautiful earth, the mountains, rivers, coastlines, parks, and quite simply a home-cooked evening meal, if we are stuck in conference rooms, cars, cubicles or operating rooms for hours on end? You might say, *Well, this is the way of the world now, people have to put in the hours to keep their jobs; besides, what if I can't find a job with better hours?* That is a non-trusting attitude. That is buying into the lies of Satan who promises more than what God can give, but he never delivers in the long term. If Satan lures you into a great paying job that requires most of your waking hours and forces you to put your family on hold for years, you will find that down the road you will sustain major disappointment, loss, or heartache. How about trusting

God? How about realizing the truth and letting God lead you to a job with better hours that you absolutely enjoy? The Bible states, "The blessing of the Lord brings wealth, without painful toil for it" (Prov 10:22 NIV). Your only sacrifice will be to sincerely follow Him. God created the world. He is all knowing, all powerful, and ever present. He knows how the world works today and what it takes to make a living. He also wants His followers to enjoy life. True joy in life comes first and foremost from a relationship with God, who guides you into meaningful work, a sane schedule, time to relax with loved ones, and time to bless others. If you are working excessively just to bring home a paycheck, take a leap of faith. You will never regret it.

HOMEWORK:
Read the lyrics while listening to "Evidence" by Citizen Way[1]

SONG VERSE TO CONTEMPLATE:
"I need hands that are open
Reaching out to broken hearts
'Cause that's the only way this world
Would ever know who You are
Love is the evidence"

GOD'S PROMISE:
"Give, and it will be given to you." (Lk 6:38 NASB)

Six

Pre-Monday

As I continued my search for the Lord outside of the Catholic tradition by reading the Bible, I decided to go to a non-denominational church that was suggested by my Christian girlfriend. The first few times I went, being there felt very foreign to me—like I was sitting in a casual lecture on faith in Jesus Christ. I was uncomfortable without the formality of Catholicism, but because I could completely relate to the pastor's message, I continued to go week after week. The messages were based on the same foundation as the Catholic beliefs I'd grown up with: Jesus died on the Cross for our salvation, and the Lord exists in the trinity of three persons. But for the first time in my life, I could actually relate to these ideas and understand how God can help me daily, how following Him is the way to a truly happy and peace-filled life. I realized that religions are man-made and that faith in God is something for all of us to receive directly from God when we read His Word. This all had much greater meaning to me. My heart and mind were wide open to this wonderful personal relationship I was developing with our Lord which lead me to want to follow the Lord's teachings as closely as possible. I started to examine my life and how I lived. Then I wondered, *Is simply going to church on Sundays enough to honor the Lord?*

Some people think of the week like this: Monday, Monday #2, Monday #3, Monday #4, Friday, Saturday, Pre-Monday! I always found this humorous, however I realized that Sunday is such an important day of the week that we are told how to live that day of the week in the Ten Commandments. They tell us to "Remember the Sabbath day, to keep it holy" (Ex 20:8). Elsewhere in the Bible we are instructed, "For six days you shall labor but on the seventh day you shall rest, in order to honor the Lord."[2] This commandment took some time for me to understand; I wasn't even sure honoring the Sabbath is still relevant today. After spending time "in the Word," as Christians say, God impressed upon my heart that this commandment is even more important today in our fast-paced society. The day becomes a joyful reminder of God at work in our lives; we *can* rest for an entire day without work. God then will assist us in completing our tasks during the remaining six days. This is a benefit for believers who follow God's teachings.

If we honor the Sabbath and do as the Bible verse says by having no one in our families do any sort of work on Sundays, this day becomes a gift. It is a set day of the week where we can spend time with the most important people in our lives: our Father in heaven and our family. Pastor Rick Warren stated, in his amazing book *The Purpose Driven Life*, that the best way to spell love is T-I-M-E.[1] When you love someone you spend time together. If we spend time with our children by reading books to them, throwing the ball around, or sitting and talking together, we are showing our children that we love them and that they are valuable to us. The same goes for our spouses; if we use Sundays as a time to have coffee together, take walks together, or engage in an activity or sport together, we are showing our spouse that we love them and that they are worth our time. The work week can be so busy that we don't have as much time for this as we would like, so Sunday is the day set apart to honor our Creator and nurture our relationships. If we are spending Sundays catching up on everything we need to do, we aren't honoring this commandment and we are missing out on love. This love is, first and foremost, the love and peace God can give us as we focus on Him. Secondly, it is the love of our children, spouses, extended family, and friends. What God is asking us to do with this commandment is to set aside one day of the week for the gifts that He gave us, so we can enjoy them and be thankful to Him. This is what life is all about.

When I grew up, most businesses were closed on Sundays. Slowly over the years, somehow this Christian commandment has been encroached upon. Not only do bosses expect some employees to work on a Sunday, but activities like club sports and other required events happen on Sundays which precludes our children from having a full day of rest. There have even been kids' golf tournaments in my town on Easter Sunday! Is this what we want as Christians, to sleepwalk through our lives and let other people change the value we place on this holy day of the week? How many of us have realized too late that our child had a game on a Sunday and we missed the opportunity to go to church? If we don't stop and honor the Lord on Sundays, they will feel like just any day of the week and they are not! What I have learned is that God deserves a recognizable day of the week—a day set apart from all of the others so that we have time to honor Him and, most importantly, to thank Him and enjoy all of our blessings. Simply put, Sunday is God's day and that should be in the forefront of our minds.

Imagine a world where every business except those related to health and public safety closed its doors to making money on Sunday. Imagine if we respected Sunday for what it truly is, God's day of rest for us. Imagine what a wonderful life it would be. Neighbors would be able to get to know each other in a relaxed and unhurried way and families could volunteer together to help out in the community, which would bless others and promote family closeness. If we, as Christians, collectively believe that killing is wrong because it is one of the Ten Commandments, why don't we honor the Sabbath? Are some commandments more important than others? Can we pick and choose? Like I said before, God gave us the Ten Commandments to make our lives free of unnecessary pain, stress, and negative consequences. Most importantly, He gave the Ten Commandments to us to protect our loving relationships. After much meditation on the subject, I finally realized that if we all honored the Sabbath (Sunday), and no one in our houses did any sort of work, we would all look forward to that day of the week. When I incorporated this into my life and spent the day going to church, cooking with my children, taking walks, and reading enjoyable, not-work-related things, we all really looked forward to the day. On Saturday night I would say, "Yeah, tomorrow is Sunday, I don't have to do anything; I am commanded not to do anything!" My children enjoy it because it is a leisurely day and they know nothing will be required of them. Honoring the Sabbath (or another day for service providers) is really about putting down our obligations for the day and enjoying the people in our lives.

Mother Theresa was once asked, "How do you promote world peace?" Her answer was, "Go home and love your family." This is quite an astute statement if you stop to think about it. Our family is the first place we feel love or rejection and this feeling can stay with us our entire lives. God wants us to be present for our families. He put this commandment on the same list as "Do not kill," perhaps because it is immensely important for our well-being. Let us all heed the words of the Lord and "Remember the Sabbath day by keeping it holy" (Ex 20:8). I hope you find Sundays to be a little slice of heaven like I do.

HOMEWORK:
Read the lyrics while listening to "Write Your Story" by Francesca Battistelli[2]

SONG VERSE TO CONTEMPLATE:
"Author of my hope
Maker of the stars
Let me be Your work of art"[2]

GOD'S PROMISE:
"And these blessings shall come upon you and overtake you, if you obey the voice of the Lord your God." (Deut 28:2)

SEVEN

LUCKY NUMBER SEVEN

"Ask and it will be given to you, seek and you will find; knock and the door will be opened to you" (Mt 7:7 NIV).

First of all, take a look at that verse number. Is there any doubt why we as a society associate the number seven with luck? This extremely hopeful verse was staring at me when I really needed some hope. *But what exactly does that mean?* I wondered, as I was negotiating my way around my new life. Can a person of faith really ask and receive? The Bible states that "anyone who comes to Him must believe that He exists and that He rewards those who earnestly seek Him" (Heb 11:6 NIV). Gosh, it's another hopeful Bible verse stating that we are rewarded for being a believer! *There must be something to this!* I thought. As I meditated on these verses of Scripture I also kept in mind that God refers to Himself as Father. I pictured this image in my mind: a patient, soft-spoken man who gently guides His children. I realized that as a mother, I always want to make my children happy—not only with things they enjoy, but with love and with our time together, too. I felt in my heart that God was saying to me, "Yes, I will give you what you ask for if it is good, if the timing is right, and if it will benefit you." The

Bible states, "If you, then, though you are evil, know how to give good gifts to your children, how much more will your Father in heaven give good gifts to those who ask Him!" (Mt 7:11 NIV).

As parents, most of us can't always do what our children want at a particular time in their life. For example, my sixteen-year-old wanted a car as soon as she got her driver's license. All of her friends received cars at sixteen, so when her birthday came, she just expected it. I told her that she didn't need a car at that time, but that she would have one when she really needed one. In the same way, God will give us the desires of our heart when we need His provision. If we are living a comfortable lifestyle yet we are extremely discontent and obsessively pray to win the lottery, I wouldn't be surprised if God is disappointed. This seems to fall under the commandment of "Do not covet." Don't get me wrong, I have joined in a pool for the lottery at work and I have entered contests for the fun of it, dreaming of money to renovate my kitchen. The question is: are we playing for fun or are we truly discontent with our current modest lifestyle? On the other hand, if we want to change jobs to be home more with our children and we are praying for a great job to fit our newfound desire to put God and family before money, this request seems more likely to be answered. Our prayers are always answered in God's timing and if they are in line with God's teachings. We also know from Scripture that our prayers are heard when we remove all known sin from our lives, because sin places a barrier between God and us. If these criteria are met, then ask away! Remember, humans have a very limited view of the world. If you are praying for something and it doesn't happen, don't let that discourage you. God doesn't arbitrarily say no. If His answer seems to be "No," it is because God knows all and He is working out your life for your good.

The ultimate prayer we can give ourselves is to say, "God, I give up control of my life. Please direct me in the way I should go." This is not a "ball and chain" type of deal; it is the freedom to live in complete trust that all of our needs will be taken care of and all the desires of our heart that God gave us will materialize when we hand our life over to God. The Bible states, "Now all glory to God, who is able, through His mighty power at work within us, to accomplish infinitely more than we might ask or think" (Eph 3:20 NLT). Following God's way brings us freedom to live free of the fear and stress that steal our joy. It is freedom to take a job we love instead of a job we hate because it has a higher income. God wants us to be happy and use our talents. We bring more joy to a job that we love than to one we hold down just for a paycheck. Giving God the "go ahead" to run your life is the key to freedom. The Bible states, "The truth will set you free" (Jn 8:32b NLT). When you know God's word (God's truth) and follow His way rather than man's way, you will have internal joy. In a word, you are *free* to live life without fear, trusting that God will work out your life in the best way possible. Humans tend to think we know what will make us happy and we chase after our ideas, but our Creator knows the Truth.

It took several years into my life as a new Christian (one who follows God's teachings and not religious rules made up by men), for me to trust God enough to run my life. I wasn't even sure I wanted that. I was worried that I wouldn't be able to have the kind of fun I was used to. I worried that God would make me give up all of my possessions like Mother Theresa. I was worried that I couldn't buy nice things for my children and myself or spend money on vacations. I didn't exactly know what was going to happen when I asked God to take over the direction for my life. Ironically, if you really stop and think about this, don't we do this when we join into marriage? We really don't know our spouses' motives or if they will always be kind, loving, truthful and dependable through thick and thin. Why do we, as human beings, trust other people with the rest of our lives more than we trust God? Why is it that a guy or a woman you met two years ago is worthy of trust and a lifelong commitment, but we are all so worried about committing our lives to our Creator, the One who only wants the best for us and wants to bless us profusely as He tells us in the Bible? After I looked at the dichotomy of the situation—trusting a fallible human being implicitly, but not trusting our sovereign God—I realized I had absolutely no fear to deal with. God wants what is best for all of us and He knows what will make each one of us happy, joyful, and at peace. The Bible states, "You will keep in perfect peace all who trust in you, all whose thoughts are fixed on you!" (Isa 26:3 NLT). We, on the other hand, are lured by Satan, the king of lies. Satan tries to entice us with ungodly behavior as well as activities and things that hold no lasting happiness. Satan's lies will lead to death: death of our joy, peace, happiness, relationships, families, and health. Satan has done a good job so far in the world; he has even been successful in religious families. But my goal is to have you say "I do" to our Father in heaven and let Him lead you into a beautiful life in His Kingdom. The Kingdom is a place where we can live without fear, completely trusting that we will always have all that we need and more as we follow God.

I am happy to report that since handing over control of my life to God several years ago, I have had more peace, ease in life, joy, time with loved ones, a higher income, and greater fulfillment in my work. Nothing, absolutely nothing, is worse for saying "I do" to God.

"Blessed are those who find wisdom,
those who gain understanding,
for she is more profitable than silver
and yields better returns than gold.
[Wisdom] is more precious than rubies;
nothing you desire can compare with her.
long life is in her right hand;
in her left hand are riches and honor.
Her ways are pleasant ways,
and all her paths are peace.
[Wisdom] is a tree of life to those who take hold of her;
those who hold her fast will be blessed"
(Proverbs 3:13-18 NIV).

This proverb sums up, once again, what is stated in so many books of the Bible. Following God's teachings gives us better returns than gold (our investments)—it gives us a long life, riches, honor, peace, and blessings. It also allows our prayers to be heard and answered. Yes, you can ask, seek, and knock; believe that God wants you to be happy and blessed with all of the enjoyable aspects of life, for this is God's truth. The Bible states, "Whoever looks intently into the perfect law that gives freedom, and continues in it—not forgetting what they have heard, but doing it—they will be blessed in what they do" (Jas 1:25 NIV).

HOMEWORK:
Read the lyrics while listening to "The Motions" by Matthew West

SONG VERSE TO CONTEMPLATE:
"I don't wanna go through the motions
I don't wanna go one more day
Without Your all consuming passion inside of me" [1]

GOD'S PROMISE:
There is nothing to fear when I am leading you.

Eight

Pacifier

As I was straddling two churches, the Catholic church I attended for years and a non-denominational Christian church, I started to assess what was being taught and modeled. For the first time in my life I didn't accept out of hand what was going on at either of these houses of God. I went to Catholic Mass and Catholic school functions with an outsider's view for the first time. It was no longer routine to me because I took the opportunity to step out of the Catholic faith to be an attender at another church. This allowed me to compare and contrast the two. The basic requirement I had in my mind was that the masses/services and functions held at each church should coincide with the Word of God. I had read countless passages of Scripture about Christians standing out in society as people with love, joy, peace, patience, kindness, gentleness, and self-control (Gal 5:22-23). In fact, the following Bible verse explains what happens when those who believe in God act differently from the way non-believers act: "The name of our Lord Jesus will be honored because of the way you live, and you will be honored along with Him" (2 Thess 1:12 NLT).

It didn't take very long for me to see a glaring difference between the churches once I began to simply compare how they each provided fun and fellowship for their congregants. For instance, I went to a family festival at the non-denominational church and saw that games, bouncy pits, rock walls, and food booths were all present. The only thing that was missing was alcohol—there wasn't a beer tent! This was different to me. Every family festival and fundraiser for the Catholic schools and church in my community incorporated alcohol to some degree, be it a beer garden or a full-out bar. The alcohol at these functions never seemed to be moderated in any way, such as a one- or two-glass limit of wine served as part of a meal. The Catholics consumed any amount of alcohol they so desired. I stopped for the first time in my life and thought about this. If our churches don't model having fun without alcohol, where exactly will our children learn that fun can be had without a drop of beer consumed? I am not opposed to modest alcohol consumption by any means; however, most Catholic high schools teach their students that drinking and driving is wrong and that alcohol isn't necessary to have fun. So by serving un-moderated alcohol at all of the fundraisers that the parents attend with the high school students present, it would appear that we are modeling the exact opposite of what we preach. The Bible teaches, "Train up a child in the way he should go; even when he is old he will not depart from it" (Prov 22:6 ESV). Whether we know it or not, we are training our children by our behavior. I think it would be a better idea if Catholic fundraising events either eliminated alcohol entirely or served wine in moderation as part of the meal. This type of consumption falls directly in line with the biblical use of alcohol. Sometimes we, myself included, forget that children watch everything we do, but they don't necessarily listen to everything we say. We can preach all we want about not drinking and driving but their young, impressionable eyes see our excessive drinking and our contradictions. If we want to teach our children in the ways of the Lord, we need to exercise some self-control in order to accomplish that. We don't want to show our children that alcohol is necessary at all times because that could lead to problems down the road. Let me show you what I mean.

Within the first year of studying the Bible, I came to the knowledge that God wants to have our sole allegiance. He wants to be number one in our life before everything else. I examined my life and the lives of the people around me and realized that most of us do not put God first. Most people have something or someone in their life that they use to get to their "happy place." Even if this something is a healthy activity, like exercising, it could become our god if we let it, meaning we are a slave to an activity, object, or person for our happiness. "Thou shalt have no other gods before me" (Ex 20:3 KJV). This means that God should be the provider of all peace and happiness in our lives and we should go to Him first when we have a need to be filled.

Is there something in your life that is excessive and you think you cannot be happy without? If you invite the Lord fully into your life, God can help you get out of temptation, dependence, or lack of control with that particular aspect of your life. Your problem, whatever it is, can be controlled once you give your life over to God. Life lived on our own accord can be very hard, not to mention painful and exhausting. If you don't know the Lord, it's easy to seek human "targets" in overabundance to try to numb the pain. But these false sights have consequences. For some people, the excess may cause weight gain, a packed closet, or a smoker's cough. For other people, the excess becomes a true addiction, our pacifier of sorts, that helps get us through the day. Let's look at alcohol as an example.

Some people need to drink the minute they get up and it destroys their entire day. Others are functional alcoholics and they can hide their need for alcohol fairly well; they only drink after all of their work is done at the end of the day. It doesn't matter whether we are able to hide our excessive behavior or not. If the behavior becomes necessary for your happiness it has to be eliminated in order to live a life in God's kingdom and enjoy His countless blessings.

As parents, we know that after a certain point in toddlerhood, the pacifier must go or it could have negative effects on a child's bite, teeth, and quite possibly, his life. There is the possibility that other kids will make fun of him if he keeps using a pacifier; there is also the possibility that relying on it could harm his self-esteem. As adults, we may not get ridiculed to our faces about our metaphorical pacifiers, but they will still ruin our lives eventually unless we get rid of them. Anything that holds our happiness keeps us in bondage; we are tethered to it like a ball and chain. Depending on the strength of our addiction, responsibilities can be neglected. When children are involved in this neglect, a whole host of problems snowballs as a consequence.

God created us to have a need—a longing, you might say—for a relationship with Him. This need was not intended for material things, substances, activities, or serial relationships. There is absolutely nothing on this earth that will take away that hollow feeling within your chest, that emptiness and lack of joy, except God. We all have seen a young, frantic child crying hysterically until he finds his pacifier. That little piece of plastic holds his happiness. Do we really want something to hold our happiness? When you turn your life over to God and sincerely wish to follow His ways, He will get you out of your bondage to your pacifier. What's ironic is that often, people feel that following the Lord will keep them in bondage to Him. I have come to realize through Bible study that by *not* taking the Lord as CEO of your life, you will be kept in bondage, seeking, searching, longing, and striving for something that will make you at peace at last. The Bible says,

"No temptation has overtaken you that is not common to man. God is faithful, and He will not let you be tempted beyond your ability, but with the temptation He will also provide the way of escape, that you may be able to endure it" (1 Cor 10:13 ESV).

Wouldn't it be easier to remove excessive alcohol from your life if church events were free of alcohol? Catholics who are recovered alcoholics can't even attend a family festival put on by the church without encountering temptation. Do you see anything wrong with this? Catholics have the right to ask questions of their church, and should make their voices heard by speaking to the principals of the Catholic schools, the priests, and most importantly, the bishops. Ask them why un-moderated alcohol is included on church grounds and within the four walls of the Catholic schools. Ask them if the Pope condones this behavior and why. Remind them that every church stands under the authority of Scripture and therefore, the church's teachings and events are to be judged by Scripture. We as Christians are "A chosen people, a royal priesthood, a holy nation, God's special possession" (1 Pet 2:9 NIV). Our Lord calls us to lifestyles that honor Him because He wants to help us and bless us with the desires of our heart. The evidence in the Bible is very clear. If you want to enter into life in God's kingdom, the place of rest and help, joy and peace, cry out to the Lord for help to get out of bondage to your pacifier. It will be the best day of your life.

"Be sober minded; be watchful. Your adversary the devil prowls around like a roaring lion, seeking someone to devour" (1 Pet 5:8 ESV).

"Wine is a mocker, strong drink a brawler, and whoever is intoxicated by it is not wise" (Prov 20:1 NASB).

"All things are lawful for me, but not all things are helpful. All things are lawful for me, but I will not be enslaved by anything" (1 Cor 6:12 ESV).

"Now the acts of the flesh are obvious: sexual immorality, impurity and debauchery; idolatry and witchcraft; hatred, discord, jealously, fits of rage, selfish ambition, dissensions, factions and envy; drunkenness, orgies, and the like. I warn you, as I did before, that those who live like this will not inherit the kingdom of God" (Gal 5:19-21 NIV).

HOMEWORK:
Read the lyrics while listening to "Here for a Reason" by Ashes Remain.[1]
Extra credit: "Voice of a Savior" by Mandissa[2]

SONG VERSES TO CONTEMPLATE:
*"Every day that your heart keeps beating
There's purpose for your life"* [1]

*"You and I are not that different
We got a void and we're just trying to fill it up"* [2]

GOD'S PROMISE:
I am here; you have my attention.

Nine

Planting

The deeper I dove into the Word of God, I couldn't help but realize how perfectly God made the world. It is too much to conceptualize with our human brains but we can take the laws of the nature as an example. God made the world with very specific laws, which we now call universal laws. These include the laws of relativity, vibration, cause and effect, and gravity. These principles that help explain our universe were created by God and are unchanging. There have been atheistic scientists who are baffled at the mathematical preciseness of these laws and simply call them miracles.

Perhaps God specifically made the law of cause and effect so that His people could have more control over their lives. In essence, the law states that if you do A, then B will happen. Scripture seems to support this law in the passage of sowing and reaping (Gal 6:7-10). Scripture states, "Don't be misled—you cannot mock the justice of God. You will always harvest what you plant" (Gal 6:7 NLT). A second verse along this line is, "Give, and it will be given to you. A good measure, pressed down, shaken together and running over, will be poured into your lap. For with the measure you use, it will be measured to you" (Lk 6:38 NIV). Both of these verses tell us that whatever we do will inevitably come back to us. The second verse makes it clear that "good measures" or kindness that we do for others out of the goodness of our hearts will come back to us. It may not be in equal portion, but because God is all good, He makes sure our good deeds come back to us "running over," in other words, in abundance. So how do we incorporate this into our lives on a consistent basis? Let's first talk about tithing.

When I started working at my first "real" job out of college, I was introduced to the word *tithing*, which is giving 10% of our income to God's Church. My first reaction to this concept was, *Wow, that is a lot of cash and I have student loans to pay off, a used car loan, and an apartment to furnish; there is no way that I can do that!* I also thought that tithing was the Church's way of laying guilt on people to pay their bills. At the time, I had no idea that tithing is actually a biblical principle. Biblical principles teach us to trust in the Word of God and when we do, God blesses us. We need to remember that God doesn't need our money. If you think about it, God could make money suddenly appear just like He did by multiplying the loaves and fish in the Bible (Mk 6:41-44). God wants us to show our belief and trust in Him by following His principles. When we trust that we will always have enough, we can then bless others with our gifts. For example, if a tornado took down your neighbor's house and your church stepped in and significantly helped her out using tithes and offerings, your neighbor might just stop and look up to the heavens and say, "God is good." The consequence to tithing doesn't end there. If we use the principle of sowing and reaping, we can feel confident that if we are giving money to help someone else out, God will supply all of our needs as well. The Bible states, "God shall supply all your needs according to His riches in glory by Christ Jesus" (Phil 4:19 NKJV). Another verse to consider when tithing is, "'Bring the whole tithe into the storehouse, that there may be food in my house. Test me on this, says the Lord Almighty, and see if I will not throw open the floodgates of heaven and pour out so much blessing that there will not be room enough to store it'"(Mal 3:10 NIV). This passage is very clear: God will supply blessings to those who obediently tithe.

I am well aware that tithing is a very hard concept. We all want a life of comfort and giving our money away seems counterintuitive. Didn't I just tell you in an earlier chapter not to seek after money with your job? Now you have less money and I am showing you that God wants you to give part of it away. This is when you will see the exceeding greatness of God. God's way of seeing our faith in Him is when He sees us do what he asks of us even when it is hard. When He sees us obey His Word for the benefit of His Church and His world, we are blessed. We aren't "maybe" blessed; you can count on being blessed as it is written. I understand that life is expensive and seems to be more expensive every year. As a believer of God though, it is worth testing this biblical principle—it will be the best investment you ever make. It will be hard to write the check every month to the church. At first it is wrenchingly hard! But after a while you will realize that you still have enough. A short time later you will realize that a few coincidences happened that you didn't expect. Maybe you landed that lucrative account, or you got a pay raise, or you got a bigger tax return than you had anticipated or you inherited money from some distant relative. The flip side to this is that you might think a little harder about the money you spend. Maybe you will realize that going out to eat mediocre food is not as good or as economical as cooking with the family at home. Maybe that gourmet coffee drink could be changed to a real coffee; this will save a few dollars and a few calories too! Whatever it is, you will see some change in your finances for the better. Trusting God pleases Him and giving in order to help others pleases Him as well. The Bible states, "Truly I tell you, whatever you did for one of the least of these brothers and sisters of mine, you did for me" (Mt 25:40 NIV). The act of tithing is a way to promote God's work in this world and as you do this, God will stretch what you have left. The fact that we are trusting God moves God to prove His faithfulness to us. When we give cheerfully and joyfully (which, by the way, takes time!), we are putting God in a position to follow up on the words He told us in the Bible. The Bible states, "God is not human, that He should lie, not a human being, that He should change His mind. Does He speak and then not act? Does He promise and not fulfill?" (Num 23:19 NIV). The promises in the Bible are sound; we can trust them.

Beyond the fear of giving money, we need to step back and see another truth. We are the hands and feet of God on this earth. This truth will help you to understand our *need* to give to others. All of the good things in our lives are blessings from God that we need to share. The Bible declares, "Every good and perfect gift is from above" (Jas 1:17 NIV). When we realize this and desire to share, God will reward us by taking care of our needs. The Bible teaches us that no one can out-give God. That lesson was learned in the very first book of the Bible, Genesis. To make a long story short, Abram (yes, that is his name!) gave his nephew Lot the best of the land so that there would be no strife between them. When God had seen what Abram did, he gave Abram every other piece of land to the North, South, East and West as far as he could see (Gen 13). Like with Abram, when God sees your generosity, He will reward you.

When you make room for tithing in your life, you may just come to the conclusion that you already have so much. This attitude of thankfulness for your richly blessed life pleases God. You are stating with your words and actions that you feel lucky to have what you currently have and because of this you can spare some income to help others. This attitude of prosperity will provide you with more. The Bible states, "Whoever has will be given more, and they will have an abundance. Whoever does not have, even what they have will be taken from them" (Mt 13:12 ESV). The second part of this verse, "Whoever does not have," means that people who don't understand God at His Word feel they don't have enough money to tithe and because of this they will always live in a state of lack, real or imagined. The "hearers" of God's message know that it is in giving that we receive.

Tithing has another requirement as far as the Bible teaches: we need to do it secretively and not boast about our tithing. The Bible states, "So when you give to the needy, do not announce it with trumpets, as the hypocrites do in the synagogues and on the streets, to be honored by others. Truly I tell you, they have received their reward in full" (Mt 6:2 NIV). Tithe in order to promote God's work in this world, not out of prideful desire to be noticed. Then wait and watch how good our God is to you for your faithfulness. The Bible states, "A generous person will prosper; whoever refreshes others will be refreshed" (Prov 11:25 NIV).

It is easier to give when we remember that everything we have comes from the Lord: our talent to make money, the parents who gave us direction, our safe childhood so we didn't grow up jaded. Everything, I repeat, *everything* good in our lives has been given to us from God. The Bible reminds us that "Everything comes from Him and exists by His power and is intended for His glory" (Rom 11:36 NLT). Let's all live in an attitude of thankfulness and use the blessings we already have in our lives to bless others. You will find that helping out in the world brings meaning and significance to your own life, and the end result of that is joy.

HOMEWORK:
Read the lyrics while listening to "Do Something" by Matthew West[1]

SONG VERSE TO CONTEMPLATE:
"I wanna be the one who stands up and says, 'I'm going to do something.'"[1]

GOD'S PROMISE:
I am faithful to those who are faithful to me.

Ten

Real-Life Examples

As I was learning about tithing and realizing for the first time that this biblical principle is a sound and valid ideal, my eyes were opened to some real-life examples. These successful companies and individuals believe in the teachings of the Bible and incorporate them into their business plans. Each one of the companies has stated, in no uncertain terms, that adhering to biblical principles has made their companies more profitable. The increase in profits has allowed these companies to impact the world in a positive way. All of them give generously of their financial resources and their time. The founders of these companies, their families, and the employees that share this belief system are inspirational to say the least. I would like to share a few of these stories with you.

Mary Kay Ash, Founder of Mary Kay Cosmetics

The late Mary Kay Ash founded Mary Kay Cosmetics in 1963 around the age of forty-five. In her book entitled *Miracles Happen*, she writes:

"Over the years, I have found that everything seems to work out if you have your life in the proper perspective:

> God first, family second and career third...I truly believe that the growth of May Kay Cosmetics has come about because the first thing we did is take God as a partner."[1]

Kay believed in the biblical principle that no one can out-give God. She would hand out $1 bills to her beauty consultants, on which she had signed her name and written "Matthew 25:14-30" (the parable of the talents). This parable explains that we are to use the money God gave us wisely and if we do, we will be given more. Essentially, the more you give the more you get. In her book, Kay also described a story where she was asked to give a speech to her church congregation, motivating it to give money to build a children's center. She told the congregation that whatever cash was put in the basket that Sunday she would match. The amount collected was just over one hundred thousand dollars! Kay was shocked at the sum of money collected and she wondered how she would quickly get a hold of an equal amount, as her assets were tied up. The very next day her son called her and told her that one of her oil investments came in and her share of the profit that month was one hundred thousand dollars.[2] Coincidence? No! God rewards those who use their money and talents for the good of others. In fact, the reason Kay started her company was to give women the chance to empower themselves to earn a decent living. Her focus was not on obtaining money but on helping women. This attitude of giving, taught in the Bible, has definitely played out for the cosmetic company. On the 45th anniversary of Mary Kay Cosmetics, the wholesale sales exceeded 2.4 billion dollars.[3] God has surely blessed Mary Kay's company.

DAVID GREEN, FOUNDER AND CEO OF HOBBY LOBBY STORES

David Green came from very humble beginnings. In his book, entitled *More Than a Hobby*, Green explains that he was one of six children born to a pastor and pastor's wife. The family was so poor at the time that they didn't even own a car. Due to the family's tight financial situation, Green started working in high school at a local five and dime in order to financially contribute to the family. He enjoyed this retail work very much and found that he was good at it. In his book, Green recalls that later in life, when he was a young store manager, he would arrive home at ten o'clock at night bone tired. He knew there must be another way to make a living than working such long days. For this reason he instituted four key ideas when he founded the Hobby Lobby craft store. These key ideas, he believes, lead to the success of his company:

1. Run your business in harmony with God's laws. This will keep you on ethical footing. Seek to please God in everything that you do.
2. Focus on people more than money.
3. Be a merchant...the rest is periphery or even a distraction.
4. Install the proper systems to support the first three. (He has chaplains on his payroll to counsel and support his employees).[4]

David Green believes that "When you take good care of your people...they stay happier, their families are happier, the whole company runs more smoothly. It's a win-win-win situation."[5]

This is the reason Hobby Lobby stores close at eight o'clock p.m. Green understood that there is a human toll from long work hours, and although other retailers (including Hobby Lobby's competitors) stay open much longer, Green kept his employees in mind when he determined his store's hours. In 1998 he got around to facing an even larger issue: should Hobby Lobby stay open on Sundays? Green writes,

> "The value of having a 'day of rest' each week is centuries old, and is not exclusively Christian... apparently there is a rhythm built into the created order—work no more than six days then take one off—that shouldn't be ignored."

Green phased in all of the stores to this "closed on Sunday" policy over the course of two years. Once all of the stores were on board with this biblical principle, the following year (2001) showed the highest percentage of profit in Hobby Lobby history. Green writes, "Once we did what we knew we were supposed to do, profits took off."[6] Today, Hobby Lobby is a $5.1 billion dollar enterprise and David Green and his wife Barbara are "the largest evangelical benefactors in the world."[7] The success of Hobby Lobby is attributed to the fact that the Greens are followers of God's teachings, which lead them to care about the welfare of their families, employees, customers, and those less fortunate. God blesses companies that follow Him.

S. Truett Cathy, Founder of Chick-fil-A

Chick-fil-A is an American fast food restaurant chain headquartered in College Park, Georgia. It is the home of the first chicken sandwich and is my favorite fast food restaurant by far. The Chick-fil-A website states that the late S. Truett Cathy instituted a personal and business philosophy based on biblical principles. These principles helped him make the decision to close on Sundays in 1946 when he opened his first restaurant.[8] On the website, Cathy stated that his decision was both practical and spiritual. He believed that all of the employees of Chick-fil-A should have the opportunity to rest and worship as they so choose on Sundays. He felt it is part of his recipe for success. In Cathy's last book, *Wealth: Is It Worth It?* he states, "If it takes seven days a week to make a living you ought to be doing something else."[9] Cathy emphasized the importance of faith and continued, "I'm a strong believer that the Bible is a roadmap for life...we have the golden rule at Chick-fil-A and we are motivated by a serving spirit."[9] "We can compete with the toughest competition said Cathy, simply because of the kindness of our people."[10] The corporate purpose at Chick-fil-A is "To glorify God by being faithful stewards of all that is entrusted to us and to have a positive influence on all who come in contact with Chick-fil-A."[10] Cathy and his wife Jeannette tithed ten percent of their income from the first days of their marriage and they have been huge philanthropists for quite some time. They established the WinShape Foundation named for its mission to shape winners. Cathy dedicated his time to needy children and fostered over 200 children through WinShape Homes. He gave over $30 million dollars in college scholarships to his employees in the past forty years and earned multiple philanthropic awards and honors. Cathy had an estimated net worth of $6.2 billion dollars.[11] In September 2014 the world lost this amazing man.

OPRAH WINFREY, MEDIA PROPRIETOR, TALK SHOW HOST, ACTRESS, PRODUCER, & PHILANTHROPIST

Most of us in America have seen *The Oprah Winfrey Show* at some point in our lives and I am no exception. I watched Oprah's show for years before she retired it, and I have also read *O: The Oprah Magazine*. Many of these shows and articles are thought provoking and life enhancing. Oprah has a desire to help people be in touch with their mind, body, and spirit, and does so with her new show called *Supersoul Sunday*.

Although many of her shows and articles are interesting to me, one of the things Oprah has said that stuck with me is her thought on tithing. She stated that when she started earning a paycheck back in her twenties, she tithed 10% of it to the church she attended every Sunday. She mentioned that her paychecks were anything but large in her early career days and after she tithed, she had very little to live on. Oprah adhered to what she was taught, not for prideful reasons, but in order to fulfill a duty to her Christian faith, which also showed her trust in the Lord. What I found interesting was that Oprah didn't come up with an excuse like most of us do to justify why we just can't follow this biblical principle at this time in our lives. She was faithful with her first paychecks.

I don't have to go on about how successful Oprah is, in part because she was a good steward of even her tiny paychecks when she was a young woman. God has allowed

Oprah the funds to bless others probably in part because He saw her great trust in Him early in her life. Today, Oprah donates more of her own money to charity than any other show business celebrity. Oprah has been listed in business week as one of the top 50 most generous philanthropists in America, giving away more than $400 million. She gave over $10 million to Katrina relief, put hundreds of black men through college, and traveled to South Africa to give gifts and school supplies to children affected by poverty and AIDS. She later started a school in Africa called the Oprah Winfrey Leadership Academy for Girls, which she sustains to this day. Oprah also has a charity called the Angel Network that has donated massive amounts of funds to charitable organizations around the world.[12]

As I mentioned before, the Bible tells us to "'Bring the whole tithe into the storehouse, that there may be food in my house, test me in this,' says the Lord Almighty, 'and see if I will not throw open the floodgates of heaven and pour out so much blessing that there will not be room enough to store it'" (Mal 3:10 NIV). It is apparent that God fulfilled this promise to these individuals, and He will also do this for you and me if we follow His teachings. May God continue to bless these and all of the unnamed people of this world, who use their money for the good of man and the glory of God.

HOMEWORK:
Read the lyrics while listening to "My Own Little World" by Matthew West.[13]

SONG VERSE TO CONTEMPLATE:
"What if there's a greater purpose?
I could be living right now
Outside my own little world" [13]

GOD'S PROMISE:
"[Do] not grow weary of doing good, for in due season [you] will reap." (Gal 6:9 ESV)

Eleven

Dog Leash?

"Come to me, all you who are weary and burdened, and I will give you rest. Take my yoke upon you and learn from me, for I am gentle and humble in heart, and you will find rest for your souls. For my yoke is easy and my burden is light" (Mt 11:28-30 NIV).

Early in my study of the Bible, I found this verse in Scripture and I didn't exactly like it. I thought, *A yoke—isn't that like a dog leash? I mean really, that doesn't sound very friendly!* Then after coming upon it again and again in my Bible reading sessions, I stopped and meditated on that verse until I could finally read it without getting tense inside! A yoke of course is made of wood, or at least it was in biblical times. It is used to keep two oxen together in order to pull a heavy load. As I thought about this, I realized God was trying to tell me that He and I could be yoked together to pull the weight of my troubles if only I would let Him completely into my life. When God is yoked to you, you can be sure He is doing 90% of the work. You will be resting in the presence of the Lord as you make your way through the valley of your life.

Unfortunately in my younger years, I never really knew that God desires to be a part of every aspect of our lives. Many people think that God is not interested in the small matters of our lives; however, this thinking is entirely wrong. We can pray about everything and the closer we are tethered to God the more our prayers will be answered—sometimes the answer is instantaneous. We must "pray continually" as it states in 1 Thessalonians 5:17 (NIV). Allow yourself to be yoked to God in the good times and bad, and you will feel an unusual lightness as you go about your tasks, schedules, and tedium.

Looking back, I had an unbelievable childhood, full of fun, friends, and family. Because of this I never sought knowledge of God. I went to church on Sundays because I had to, and when I didn't have to (i.e. when I went to college) I didn't go. I was never one to attend church in order to look like a good person or to fulfill a religious obligation; I needed to learn something or else I felt I was wasting my morning. At the time, I didn't know that going to church with a heart open to learning is one of the many ways of honoring the Lord. Note that I said a heart *open* to God—this wasn't always the case with me. I went to church, said the memorized prayers, sat, stood, and kneeled at the appropriate times, and felt content that I was doing the right thing. In Isaiah 29:13 (NLT) the Lord says, "These people say they are mine. They honor me with their lips, but their hearts are far from me. And their worship of me is nothing but man-made rules learned by rote." BINGO! That was me. I am thankful, however, that I had parents who took me to the local church because I was raised with knowledge of

God, who was available to help us when needed. I had a true faith that God existed but He gave me such a great life that I never felt the need to pray unless I wanted something. Not having read the wisdom of the Bible, I never knew that there were so many ways God could help out in our lives, and more importantly, use us for His glory. Our Father in heaven wants to be included in our lives. He wants to guide us in the big decisions and the little decisions. He doesn't want us to have to backtrack and waste time. He wants us to live powerful lives through Him and for Him. This requires us to invite Him in by spending time in His presence and reading His word.

Getting started with the Bible in your lap seems daunting; where should one begin? I feel that it is easiest to get started in the Psalms or Proverbs. The Book of Psalms was written by several authors but King David (as in David and Goliath) wrote the majority of them. They touch on a wide variety of problems and human emotions, and all of us can find several Psalms that fit how we are feeling at any moment. They help us know that King David felt exactly the same way we do and that we too, can cry out to the Lord in pain and He will comfort us. The majority of the Book of Proverbs was written by King Solomon. The Proverbs help to keep us on track by reminding us of the consequences for being impulsive and living outside the will of God (for example, giving in to that feeling of anger instead of stepping back and waiting to discuss things after we have cooled down). Other Proverbs compare God's way versus man's way. Both the book of Psalms and Proverbs are great starting points when reading the Bible. I now consult the Bible on absolutely every decision I make; all decisions are first prayed about and then I open the Bible for some quiet reading time. I never fail to get an answer to my question. For example, I am a freelance worker, so my work opportunities come in spurts. I had a dry spell for several months with very sparse work and my finances were getting extremely tight. I was pondering the thought of signing a full time contract to be a regular employee, but this decision would have required extra time away from my children due to the extra hours. I was torn: I would get paid vacation time, a regular paycheck, and other perks, but as a single mom I just didn't feel right seeing my kids less just for extra (albeit much needed) money. I sat down with the Bible in my lap and said, *God, I am thinking of signing a contract to make a more stable income and I was wondering what you thought about this.* I opened up the Bible and was amazed with the verse my finger landed upon, "Be content with your wages" (Lk 3:14b NKJV). Wow, had I read that right? I was given an exact verse for my question! I gathered my kids around the Bible and showed them. (My sixteen year-old was not pleased; she had just gotten her license and wanted a car. Even a used one, she said, would be okay!). I then remembered that God wants us to seek His kingdom first and not money. The increased workload would have taken time away from my children and encroached on all of the time I spend reading Christian literature and the Bible. God also knew that several months down the road, two full-time employees would be putting in their resignations. Now I can continue to work the hours that are best for my family, and my financial situation is back on track. I also realized that

God was keeping me in control of my time so that I could write this book.

During the waiting period when I was not working very many hours, I also felt lead by God to break off a dating relationship that was not following the teachings of the Lord and took up some of my free time. I again asked God a question: *What should I do with all of my free time, Lord?* He answered me immediately—not out loud, but deep in my soul—with this sentence: "Put together all of that knowledge." The knowledge He was speaking of was everything I have learned from poring over the Bible and Christian literature for the past decade or so; I then knew that I needed to share it in a book. Times like these, direct answers to prayers and questions that I have posed to God, remind me that God is helping all of His followers and desires to be an active part of our lives.

As my new life unfolded and I was sticking with my part-time work status to spend time with my children, I was at peace and I knew God would provide enough work to cover all of my obligations. The Bible says, "Those who trust in the Lord will find new strength. They will soar high on wings like eagles. They will run and not grow weary" (Isa 40:31 NLT). Every morning when I wake up I go straight to my knees, thanking God for all of my blessings and asking for direction, help, and guidance in my job and with my home and parental duties. Most mornings I drink coffee and read the Bible for 20-30 minutes—even on the days I wake up at 4:30am for work. When I do this, I seem much more efficient with my time and get all of my tasks accomplished and more. When I skip my Bible reading time, my day seems fragmented and I feel lazy. Coincidence? I hardly think so. God can expand your time, energy, and money as He sees fit. He knows what you have to accomplish and if you put Him first even though your schedule is full, you will be rewarded. This is a fact I have come to know and experience. So I am asking you to give your burden to God. Take His yoke upon your neck and learn from Him about how to live your life; you will be so thankful you did.

HOMEWORK:
Read the lyrics while listening to "Oceans" (Where Feet May Fail) by Hillsong United[1]

SONG VERSE TO CONTEMPLATE:
"Spirit lead me where my trust is without borders"[1]

GOD'S PROMISE:
Call on me and I will show you the way to go.
(Jer 33:3; Ps 32:8)

Twelve

Time Out

"Consider it pure joy, my brothers and sisters, whenever you face trials of many kinds" (Jas 1:2 NIV).

When I first read this verse in the Bible, I breezed over it because it just didn't make sense to me. Consider it fun to be in "time out?" Consider it a blast that I am getting what I thought was an undeserved spanking at this point in my life? To say this was a hard one to grasp would be putting it mildly. However, God waits to give us understanding until we are ready. When I finally saw bits of a rainbow peeking into my life during my difficult years (such as beneficial coincidences as the hand of God), God probably said, "Okay, I think she is ready to grasp this one." I will share with you what I learned so that you too may look at trials, tests, or extremely negative situations in your life as a way to draw you to the best life for yourself: the one God wants for you.

To give you some background information, I will tell you that not only was my family blown apart by an injustice in my life, I also lost all of my friends and my health took a turn that required me to stay home much of the time due to frequent migraines. I went from having a full social life, respect in my circle of friends, and a great income, to the opposite. Every aspect of my life changed, yet I was to consider this pure joy? Well, several years since the start of my life-altering experience, I stopped and realized that without this horrible situation I never would have stepped outside my religion and dug deeply into the Word of God to find hope. Without this hope I wouldn't understand God's wisdom. I would have missed out on experiencing His peace and power within me and I wouldn't view the world as I do now. My relationship with our Lord has given me lasting peace, countless blessings, contentment, joy, and children who love learning about how great our God is. I also wouldn't be the person I have come to be and I like how God has molded me. Yes, I can say that going through this tough terrain positively transformed my life. Needless to say, however, if God gave me the opportunity to escape my pain I would have taken Him up on it; He didn't and I am better for it.

As I was poring over the Bible one day I came to a verse that says, "To all who mourn...He will give a crown of beauty for ashes, a joyous blessing instead of mourning, festive praise instead of despair. In their righteousness, they will be like great oaks that the Lord planted for His own glory" (Isa 61:3 NLT). To me, this verse means that if you stay in faith following God's teachings, knowing He can turn it all around, God will take what was meant to destroy you and turn it into a blessing that you never saw coming and it will be better than you could ever come up with for yourself. They key of course is to have an unshakable faith that God can, and will help us if we don't take matters into our own hands to try and vindicate ourselves. No, you can't take a "Louisville Slugger to both headlights and slash a hole in all four tires!"[1] If you do that, God will not step in to help. The Lord says, "Do not take revenge, my dear friends, but leave room for God's wrath, for it is written: 'It is mine to avenge; I will repay,' says the Lord" (Rom 12:19 NIV). I can tell you that even now, my primary prayer has not been answered. God did tell me within the first few months of my life-altering experience that I would triumph; I just have to wait for His timing. How did God tell me this? Well, one night when it looked as if the power opposing me was stronger, more conniving, and better versed in getting around the law, I had the distinct feeling I was going to be buried alive by lies. At three o'clock one morning I awoke out of a dead sleep and jumped out of bed crying, "Oh my God, there is no hope!" A whisper entered my head that said, "Why do you think you are going to lose?" and "Do not be afraid." I realized at that moment that God was more powerful than what opposed me and I would eventually win if I continued to stay close to Him. I felt immediate peace wash over me and went right back to sleep. But now, many years later, a question still stands: why is God taking so long to vindicate me? Well, in my situation there are a lot of people involved. By answering my prayer, other innocent people will have their lives altered in a negative way. It took a while for me to accept that, but as I searched my heart for the reason why I had to be the one to suffer the delay, I understood that this was what was best for everyone involved, even me. The Bible says,

"But in that coming day no weapon turned against you will succeed. You will silence every voice raised up to accuse you. These benefits are enjoyed by the servants of the Lord; their vindication will come from me. I, the Lord, have spoken!" (Isa 54:17 NLT).

Along the rough terrain I have learned so much. I know the pain I have suffered was a small price to pay for my newfound relationship with God and joy-filled life. Never in a million years would I have thought that a delayed answer to my prayer would be a gift. As I was writing the bibliography for this book, I found this Bible verse, Jer 15:19, which states, "If you extract the precious from the worthless, you will become My spokesman" (NASB). Ironic. After studying the Word of God for so many years, I have come to know that God answers prayers in one of three ways:

Yes.

Yes, but not now.

No, because I have something better for you.

Stay hopeful, put your baseball bat away, and remember this verse from the Bible: "'For I know the plans I have for you,' declares the Lord, 'plans to prosper you and not to harm you, plans to give you hope and a future'" (Jer 29:11 NIV). Placing God as the first priority in your life and following His teachings puts you in a position to receive not only your answered prayer, but more wisdom and greater blessings. "Do not be afraid or discouraged...for the battle is not yours, but God's" (2 Chr 20:15 NLV).

HOMEWORK:
Read the lyrics while listening to "Shackles" by Mary Mary.[2]

SONG VERSE TO CONTEMPLATE:
"I have been down for so long
Feel like the hope is gone
But as I lift my hands, I understand
That I should praise you through my circumstance" [2]

GOD'S PROMISE:
I will never leave you; your needs will be taken care of.

Thirteen

That's Life

"You will keep in perfect peace all who trust in you, all whose thoughts are fixed on you!" (Isa 26:3 NLT).

We all encounter unfair things in life that knock us off balance and test our faith in God. Many times our first reaction is to be very angry at God. This is wasted energy. The best thing we can do when a situation like this comes up is to remember that although life is not fair, God is. What exactly does this mean? It means that although a circumstance may have ended in an egregiously unfair result, you can be sure, as a follower of God, that God will work out the outcome in your favor. There is a parable in the Bible about a persistent widow in Luke 18:3-7 that states:

"There was a widow in that town who kept coming to [the judge] with a plea, 'Give me justice against my adversary.' For some time he refused. But finally he said to himself, 'Even though I don't fear God or care what people think, yet because this widow keeps bothering me, I will see that she gets justice...' And the Lord said, 'Listen to what the unjust judge says. And will not God bring about justice for His chosen ones, who cry out to him day and night? Will He keep putting them off? I tell you, He will see that they get justice...'" (NIV).

Staying true to the Lord when the wrong thing is happening to you is probably one of the hardest things to do in your Christian walk. We all have to remember that giving up won't get us anywhere. Stay in faith that our Lord will make sure justice is served. Isaiah 35:4 states, "Say to those with fearful hearts, 'Be strong, and do not fear, for your God is coming to destroy your enemies. He is coming to save you'" (NLT). This is a biblical promise. God may turn your situation around immediately or He may take years, like He has in my situation. If He is asking you to wait He will help you through the waiting process with peace, happiness, and the security of knowing that eventually, when His timing is perfect, justice will be served. I discovered the parable of the Persistent Widow (Luke 18:1-8; also called the parable of the Unjust Judge) early on in my painful years and I knew immediately that I needed to be persistent in prayer and wait for God's timing. This has not been a cakewalk! There have been turbulent times along the way caused by well-meaning people who were trying to help but actually did the opposite. I found a verse in the Bible to deal with these people: "Father, forgive them, for they know not what they do" (Lk 23:34 ESV). When I said these words out loud during a time of no support, I was at peace. Waiting fourteen years while searching Scripture for verses that pertain to my situation have given me unshakable faith that God's Word will come to pass because God cannot lie. The Bible states, "God is not human, that He should lie, not a human being, that He should change His mind. Does He speak and then not act?

Does He promise and not fulfill?" (Num 23:19 NIV). Another favorite verse of mine tells us to "Commit everything you do to the Lord; trust Him and He will help you: He will make your innocence radiate like the dawn and the justice of your cause will shine like the noonday sun. Be still in the presence of the Lord and wait patiently for Him to act. Do not fret about people who prosper or fret about their wicked schemes." (Ps 37:5-7 NLV). We need to remember that God knows who is in the right and He will walk beside those who are mistreated, helping in all situations. The Bible states, "For the eyes of the Lord move to and fro throughout the earth that He may strongly support those whose heart is completely His" (2 Chr 16:9 NASB). He will keep you in peace. He will also make other situations in your life turn out in your favor so that as you are waiting for justice to be served, you are resting in the peace and help of our Lord and provider. In due time, all of the promises listed in the twenty-eighth chapter of Deuteronomy will be yours. I urge you to wait in faith. "But if you carefully obey His voice and do all that I say, then I will be an enemy to your enemies and an adversary to your adversaries" (Ex 23:22 ESV). These are powerful and truthful words found in the Holy Bible. Always turn to God for help during a time of crisis and He will step in to help. God cannot bear a burden unless you ask Him—remember that He gave us a free will, meaning He will stay out of your life unless you invite Him in. "Call upon me in the day of trouble; I will deliver you, and you will honor me" (Ps 50:15 NIV). This reflects back on taking God's yoke upon your neck. God will carry your burden with you and when He helps you, He pulls more than half of the weight. In any unfair situation, you can turn to God. Our job is to pray and stay on the path of integrity. You won't be perfect, but every day is a new day to try again. Having an attitude of faith can bring the latter part of your life to be far better that the early years of your life. The Bible states, "'The glory of this present house will be greater than the glory of the former house,' says the Lord Almighty. 'And in this place I will grant peace'" (Hag 2:9 NIV). Never give up on your life because you were given an unfair advantage. God can make it up to you. He makes sure all of His true followers are blessed abundantly. Stay faithful, and justice will be revealed. The Bible says that "The Lord is slow to anger and great in power, and the Lord will by no means leave the guilty unpunished" (Nah 1:3a NASB).

HOMEWORK:
Read the lyrics while listening to "Voice of Truth" by Casting Crowns.[1]

SONG VERSE TO CONTEMPLATE:
"The voice of truth says, 'Do not be afraid!' And the voice of Truth says, 'This is for my glory'"[1]

GOD'S PROMISE:
I will make it up to you and give you beauty for ashes.
(Isa 61:3)

Fourteen

Forgiveness

Okay, bear with me on this one. I *know* this is a tough subject. I actually detested the word "forgive" for a long time. I knew, however, as a Christian and a person who wanted to follow all of God's teachings, that I had to do this for all of the people who destroyed my life as I knew it. I learned from Scripture that forgiveness is powerful and it's a blessing to the forgiver, so let's break it down and tackle this subject.

Does forgiveness mean we should say, *Oh golly, what you did wasn't that bad?* No! Forgiveness is not about the person or people who harmed us. It is about loving ourselves enough to want to live a happy life again. In order to get started on this path to forgiveness, it is essential to try and "walk a mile" in the shoes of the guilty. This may help you figure out why a person acted in a particular manner. Some people act out of pride or a sense of power, or because they suffered a deep hurt in their life. Other people act in ways that are disturbing to a healthy-minded person and no one is really sure why. Ask yourself: would a healthy-minded person act that way? If not, is this person actually really messed up? We all know that people can look perfectly put together on the outside and be hiding very evil secrets on the inside. Evil is a learned behavior from the devil's influence on this world. People are born beautiful, naturally friendly, trusting, and kind. This is how God made us. So if a person is acting in a manner deviant from the norm, the logical question is, "Who messed him or her up?" When you start to look at the wrongdoer as having been a victim at some time in his/her life, you can start to make a little sense of your own situation. It is best to remember that seemingly normal people could have suffered some type of trauma early in life. Many people think that kids are resilient (or at least seem to be), and therefore they will get over any wicked thing that has happened to them. I have discovered that trauma that is not dealt with will eventually emerge as some sort of sin acted out in a variety of ways. During our upbringing, anyone who had power over us when we were children could have mistreated us, leaving us with a gaping hole. This hole, if left to fester, never amounts to good. A person might engage in a self-destructive behavior as a consequence of his or her mistreatment, or he/she might perpetrate the same kind of act onto someone else. In a worst case scenario, the victim might eventually crack and perform a violent act onto someone else—an act like those that we read about in the newspaper. It is best to remember that people aren't naturally cruel, and knowing this is a good first step toward healing and forgiveness.

God created us with the Holy Spirit inside each of us to guide us along the right path in life. God also gave us a free will. This free will allows us to act in any way we see fit. Many people use their free will for good and other people use their free will to act badly toward themselves or others. There are still other people who live life unconsciously, totally unaware that the choices they make really hurt others. Free will is the reason why there is pain in the world—sometimes excruciating pain. This is a hard concept to understand. There are countless innocent victims in this world who have suffered atrocious acts of violence that test even the strongest Christian's faith. The only way to look at this is that God gave us all freedom to live close to Him or to be influenced by Satan and live as we please. With Satan influencing us, we can hurt other people. Until the Lord returns there will be violence, cruelty, and terrible injustice in the world. As Christians, the way to protect ourselves from further suffering caused by injustice is to forgive. It's worth mentioning again that I abhorred that concept for years. When I came across Scripture that said "If you forgive those who sin against you, your heavenly Father will forgive you" (Mt 6:14 NLT), I would say to myself, *Really? I need to forgive this?* Slowly (and I mean slowly!), God opened up my mind and helped me understand that forgiveness was a gift to me. My reality wouldn't change by forgiving or not forgiving; I still had my life to live. But by letting the offense go, I gained power. I had to take tiny bits of Scripture one day at a time and try my hardest to open my heart. Days turned to weeks, which turned to months, and then to years. Finally, after about six years, I was able to forgive the person who altered my life and the lives of my children. I have come to a point where I think about that person and wonder just what kind of childhood he had that caused him to have no empathy, no conscious, and no true kindness within himself to do such a thing. I started to understand that the wrongdoer is a hurting soul, separated from God. Instead of seeing him as having the upper hand in the situation, I realized that he was actually far worse off. I also realized that the upper hand of the enemy lasts only as long as God allows it to; then justice will be served. "For I, the Lord, love justice" (Isa 61:8a NIV).

Spend some time understanding the concept of forgiveness. Don't give yourself a timetable—it may take months or even several years to come to the decision to forgive. When you do finally realize that it is best for you, you will be taking your power back. In the book *Power Vs, Force,* author David Hawkins, M.D., Ph.D. writes, "The only way to enhance one's power in the world is by increasing ones integrity, understanding and capacity for compassion."[1] It is interesting to note that there is another side to forgiveness: un-forgiveness. Un-forgiveness is malice, and has been shown to make us sick. Hawkins also writes, "We are always victims of our own vindictiveness. Even secret hostile thoughts result in a psychological attack on one's own body."[2] We have a choice, then. We can either let a devastating incident ruin the rest of our lives, or we can choose to use it to make ourselves better people.

In an Associated Press column for the *New York Times*, an article featured Louis Zamperini, an Olympic track star turned prisoner of war. Zamperini was a pilot in World War II when his B-24 bomber crashed into the Pacific Ocean. After surviving 47 days on a life raft in shark-infested waters, Zamperini was captured and placed in a Japanese prison camp. He survived the worst: starvation, psychological torture, and beatings. When he was finally liberated, Zamperini was filled with rage and struggled with alcoholism and depression. Years later he became a Christian through a Billy Graham revival which changed his heart. This change allowed him to forgive one of his most horrific tormentors, and he actually wrote a letter of forgiveness to this prison guard. Thankfully, most of us won't go through such an intense, horrific situation. What I am trying to illustrate is when we turn to God and ask for help, He will change our hearts, our lives, and our entire perspective. He will make forgiveness, which may seem impossible, possible. We all have just one life to live, and it's a beautiful life. Please let God help you through your extremely painful seasons so that you can go on and make the most of the rest of your life. As the Bible states, "You intended to harm me, but God intended it for good to accomplish what is now being done" (Gen 50:20 NIV). The act of forgiving is difficult, very difficult, but worthwhile.

HOMEWORK:
Read the lyrics while listening to "Forgiveness" by Matthew West[3]

SONG VERSE TO CONTEMPLATE:
"Let it go and be amazed
By what you see through eyes of grace
The prisoner that it really frees is you."[3]

GOD'S PROMISE:
I will bless the merciful. (Mt 5:7)

Fifteen

Closing

In closing, I ask you to use this little book of wisdom to step out of your religious routine and start a relationship with our Lord. Reading the Bible while searching for God's truths and promises will help you create a better life for yourself and your family. Set aside some time each morning to read God's wisdom. As you seek Him sincerely, the Bible will begin to make sense to you and you will start to see how God wants to help you. By removing God from His "Sunday only" position and bringing Him into your everyday life, you will be taking on a strong, faithful, loving partner that will always be with you, guiding you daily to the best that life has to offer. Not only that, a relationship with God is the only way He can reveal your true purpose in life. So call out to God and invite Him into your heart. God's arms have been wide open, hoping you will run into them and experience all the blessings and peace He has for you, and He wants you today, just the way you are! Remember, "Faith is the confidence in what we hope for and assurance about what we do not see" (Heb 11:1 NIV). In a nutshell, have faith that God wants to bless the rest of your life.

HOMEWORK:
Read the lyrics while listening to "Something in the Water" by Carrie Underwood.[1]

SONG VERSE TO CONTEMPLATE:
"Was blind but now I see."[1]

GOD'S PROMISE:
Draw near to me and I will draw near to you.
(Jas 4:8)

THE END

*"So now from this mad passion
Which made me take art for an idol and a king
I have learnt the burden of error that it bore
And what misfortune springs from man's desire...
The world's frivolities have robbed me of the time
That I was given for reflecting upon God"*

– Michelangelo

Acknowledgements

My sincerest thanks go to those who helped me compile this book. Jennifer Arbaugh, my freelance editor, spent countless hours reviewing my manuscript with each change I made, all while pursuing her Master's degree. My dear friend and Christian sister, Cheryl Robinson, selflessly gave her time and effort to read the manuscript and offer suggestions. And my daughters lived through many requests to listen to a sentence or paragraph and critique the flow of my writing.

Lastly, I would like to thank our Father in heaven, who literally dropped this book into my head one day while I pondered what to do with my life. Being chosen for this project is humbling to say the least, and it reminds me that God doesn't call the qualified—rather, He qualifies the called.

I pray that this book helps Catholics realize there is more to learn about our amazing Lord beyond Sunday Mass.

Discussion Guide

1. **ABUNDANCE**
   Look up the world *abundance*. What areas of your life feel abundant right now? What areas are lacking in abundance?

   Why would our heavenly Father want His followers to live in abundance?

   How can you create abundance in your finances, free time, and family time?

2. **DAILY LIFE**
   How can you represent the Lord well through your daily routine? Think about manners, the way you dress, where you spend your time, the shows you watch, and the way you treat others.

   What could you do differently this week to show that you are a true follower of Christ?

   Share three ways you could show your devotion to the Lord during your daily routine tomorrow.

3. **Forgiveness**

    God commands us to turn the other cheek when we are hurt by others (Matt 5:39). When have you turned the other cheek?

    When might turning the other cheek not be appropriate? Is there a way you can respond in a Godly way without simply letting the same incidents happen again?

    How can you continue to be a strong Christian while standing up for yourself? Is there a time you have done this in the past?

4. **God's Laws**

    Review the Ten Commandments. Discuss how these commandments help us create strong, loving relationships.

    What does it mean to you to keep the Sabbath day holy? What could you do differently to fulfill this commandment?

    When God's laws seem to conflict with the world we live in, do you think it benefits you to follow Him anyway?

5. **Family**

    In a society with long work hours and hectic schedules, it's easy for us to lose track of time spent with our families. How do you prioritize your family?

What could you do differently this week to show your family that they are valuable to you?

Do you think there are different seasons in a person's life that demand our focus to be very narrow, such as just work and family? Do you try to do it all? Do you think your family suffers because of this?

6. **MATERIALISM**

   As Christians, we are called to share our time, money, and talents. What can you give up to share more of these with the world?

   When Americans travel to Europe they notice how small and minimalistic the homes, meals, closets, and cars are. When Europeans come to America they are amazed that everything is so much bigger. When is having more better? When might having more be a burden?

   What might you be able to part with to clear out your life and allow more time for what you value? Do you think this will ease some of your stress?

Notes

INTRODUCTION

1. Hawkins, David R. *Power vs. Force: The Hidden Determinants of Human Behavior.* Opening page.

CHAPTER ONE: GREEN GIANT

1. Mandisa. "Overcomer." *Overcomer.* Sparrow Records, 2013. CD.

CHAPTER TWO: ABUNDANCE

1. TobyMac. "Lose My Soul." *Portable Sounds.* ForeFront Records, 2007. CD.

CHAPTER THREE: THE "OLDEN" DAYS

1. Sanctus Real. "Lead Me." *Pieces of a Real Heart.* Sparrow Records, 2010. CD.

CHAPTER FOUR: TARGET PRACTICE

1. Tolle, Eckhart. *A New Earth Awakening to Your Life's Purpose.* New York: Penguin Group, 2006). Pg. 9.

2. Bremnes, Dan. "Beautiful." *Where the Light is.* Sparrow Records, 2014. CD.

Chapter Five: Presents

1. Citizen Way. "Evidence." *Love is the Evidence.* Fair Trade Records, 2013. CD.

Chapter Six: Pre-Monday

1. Warren, Rick. *The Purpose Driven Life.* Zondervan, 2002, Grand Rapids Michigan. p.12.
2. Battistelli, Francesca. "Write Your Story." *If We're Honest.* Word Entertainment and Fervent Records, 2014. CD.

Chapter Seven: Lucky Number Seven

1. West, Matthew. "The Motions." *Something to Say.* Sparrow Records, 2008. CD.

Chapter Eight: Pacifier

1. Ashes Remain. "Here for a Reason." Fair Trade Services, 2014.
2. Mandisa. "Voice of a Savior." *True Beauty.* Sparrow Records 2007. CD.

Chapter Nine: Planting

1. West, Matthew. "Do Something." *Into The Light.* Sparrow Records, 2012. CD.

Chapter Ten: Real-Life Examples

1. Ash, Mary Kay. *Miracles Happen.* 3rd Ed. HarperCollins, 1994, New York, NY, p. 60.
2. Ash, Mary Kay. *Miracles Happen.* 3rd Ed. HarperCollins, 1994, New York, NY. p. 138-44.

3. Ash, Mary Kay. *The Mary Kay Way.* John Wiley & Sons, Inc., 2008, Hoboken, New Jersey.

4. Green, David. *More Than a Hobby.* Thomas Nelson, Inc., 2005, Nashville, TN. p. 11.

5. Green, David. *More Than a Hobby.* Thomas Nelson, Inc., 2005, Nashville, TN. p.141.

6. Green, David. *More Than a Hobby.* Thomas Nelson, Inc., 2005, Nashville, TN. p. 136

7. Withnall, Adam. "Hobby Lobby: Who is David Green? 9 Facts Telling You Everything You Need to Know About the Evangelical Entrepreneur." *Independent.co.uk.* 1 July 2014. Retrieved from http://www.independent.co.uk/news/world/americas/hobby-lobby-who-is-david-green-9-facts-telling-you-everything-you-need-to-know-about-the-evangelical-9576189.html.

8. http://www.npr.org/2014/09/08/346879504/chick-fil-a-founder-credited-his-success-to-christian-principles

9. Cathy, S. Truett. *Wealth: Is It Worth It?* Looking Glass Books, Inc., 2011, Decatur, GA. p.70

10. www.chick-fil-A.com

11. Cathy, S. Truett. *Wealth: Is It Worth It?* Looking Glass Books, Inc., 2011, Decatur, GA. pp. 117

12. www.chick-fil-A.com

13. "Oprah Winfrey." *PhilanthropicPeople.com.* 2015.Retrieved from

http://www.philanthropicpeople.com/profile/oprah-winfrey/.

14. West, Matthew. "My Own Little World." *Story of Your Life.* Sparrow Records, 2010. CD.

CHAPTER ELEVEN: DOG LEASH?

1. Hillsong United. "Oceans (Where Feet May Fail)." *Zion.* Hillsong Australia, 2013. CD.

CHAPTER TWELVE: TIME OUT

1. Underwood, Carrie. "Before He Cheats." *Some Hearts.* Arista Records, 2005. CD.

2. Mary Mary. "Shackles." *Thankful.* Columbia records, 2000. CD.

CHAPTER THIRTEEN: THAT'S LIFE

1. Casting Crowns. "Voice of Truth." *Casting Crowns.* Beach Street Records, 2003. CD.

CHAPTER FOURTEEN: FORGIVENESS

1. Hawkins, David R. *Power vs. Force: The Hidden Determinants of Human Behavior.* p. 284.

2. Hawkins, David R. *Power vs. Force: The Hidden Determinants of Human Behavior.* p. 220.

3. West, Matthew. "Forgiveness." *Into the Light.* Sparrow Records, 2012. CD.

CHAPTER FIFTEEN: CLOSING

1. Underwood, Carrie. "Something in the Water." *Greatest Hits Decade #1.* Arista Nashville, 2014. CD.

About the Author

L.A. Lemke is an accidental writer, coming to the profession after twenty-four years of work in advanced practice nursing. When not writing or giving anesthetics, Lemke spends time cooking, being with her daughters, and walking her two dogs.

Follow Lemke's blog at www.biblicalwisdomonline.com/.

www.ingramcontent.com/pod-product-compliance
Lightning Source LLC
Chambersburg PA
CBHW070630300426
44113CB00010B/1720